THROUGH the WOODS

The English Woodland – April to April

H. E. Bates

Illustrated by
Agnes Miller Parker

LITTLE TOLLER BOOKS

This paperback edition published in 2011 by
Little Toller Books
Lower Dairy, Toller Fratrum, Dorset DT2 OEL

First published in 1936 by Victor Gollancz Ltd

ISBN 978-1-908213-02-0

Typeset in Monotype Sabon by Little Toller Books
Printed in India by Imprint Press

All papers used by Little Toller Books
are natural, recyclable products made from
wood grown in sustainable, well-managed forests

A CIP catalogue record for this book is available
from the British Library

5 7 9 8 6

CONTENTS

ENGRAVINGS ON WOOD

INTRODUCTION

Laura Beatty

'THERE IS', Bates muses at the end of *Through the Woods*, 'some precious quality brought about by the close gathering together of trees into a wood that defies analysis.'

So what is it? What makes a wood? More precisely, since the actual woods of Bates' acquaintance are very different from each other, what do such distinct places have to do with 'The English Woodland' of his subtitle? One is the compromised wood of his childhood in Northamptonshire, a 'paradise of primroses' through which the roar of passing trains smashes at regular intervals, and the other is the soft chestnut wood of his choosing, where the light falls on quiet and whose trees stand in pools of bluebells. How, or even why, would you reconcile such difference? What do we mean by that potent, recognisable generic that we so often invoke, and to which you can apply the definite article with such confidence, the woodland that all of us carry around in our heads? Because woods are very deep in our consciousness; they are our place of forage and shelter but also our place of trial and growth and horror at ourselves or of others, our resource and our repository. They are the place that both our food and our stories come from.

These are the questions that *Through the Woods* revolves, quietly and at the back of its mind, as it climbs the slow spiral of a year, from April to April. What are woods in themselves and what are they to us?

You won't for instance, Bates is clear, get a wood just by planting a series of trees, and in particular you won't get one by planting the same type of tree. 'There must be,' he says, 'all kinds of trees, all kinds of flowers and creatures, a conflicting and yet harmonious pooling of life.' That is Bates' recipe, variety and conflict and harmony.

When he was a child, Bates wanted for a while to be a painter. He had a box of oil paints and took lessons from a lady on the other side of the street, producing with great enthusiasm pictures of 'horrific badness'. Later, when he discovered writing, he maintained that it was 'as much a graphic art as drawing'. 'Words,' he said, were themselves 'a form of paint'. And that is, at face value, how his writing works. It is vividly descriptive, to the point where Bates is sure enough of his art to lay out his word-wood before us and simply invite us in. 'The wood is not far from the house. . . .We might as well go straight down to it.'

If we follow him we find a wood that we can see and taste and smell, that closes over our heads with its loose canopy and its slim trunks and its patterns of light closely observed and reconstructed, a wood full of slow change, of a procession of leaves and flowers, rustling with the footfall of unseen creatures. The present tense observations have the immediate, just noticed feel of a real walk in a real wood, the slightly tranced, leisurely noticing of sudden tricks of light. Honeysuckle is 'unbuttoning among the wood ridings'; in summer there are canopies of 'sun-metallic leaves'; in winter it is fallen leaves that are conjured up, the chestnut like 'ragged scraps of fawn paper', the beech 'like copper shavings', poplar and sycamore 'flat and slippery yellow fish'. And without their leaves, oaks are 'leather-budded' and the elm has 'little fluffy French knots of dark pink wool securely sewn on the jagged branches'.

In fact Bates didn't have the time to follow the year round as he wrote. The book was commissioned just after he had started contributing to the *Spectator* in 1935, and came out in 1936. In only a couple of cases the chapters are re-workings of those articles. Otherwise everything that looks like careful observation, 'nature writing', is in fact done from memory, from a painterly susceptibility to the look of things, practised subconsciously and for long enough to become deep knowledge.

When he realised he wasn't going to be a painter, Bates became a novelist. It wasn't just that his paintings were bad, they probably weren't. It was that words were better at doing what he wanted to do. He had too many different things to say for the medium of paint.

Bates was born in Rushden, in Northamptonshire in 1905, a county short on woods then, and even shorter now. His father worked in the shoe factory across the street and his grandfather, a hand-stitching cobbler by trade who couldn't face church and couldn't face factory work, took up the offer of a smallholding on a particularly intractable piece of clayland that lay at the edge of the growing town, and worked that instead. There was no trap, no form of transport apart from an old wheelbarrow. There were no farm buildings, just the great flat field, so Bates' father and grandfather had to make the piggery, the sheds, the stable and the barn themselves on Saturday mornings when the factory was closed.

This was the beginning of what Bates called 'my love and feeling for the English countryside.' It was 'out of this very ordinary, unprepossessing piece of Midland earth,' he remembers later, that there sprang up 'a paradise that remains to this day, utterly unblemished, a joy forever.'

In fact Bates' upbringing, like his writing on closer inspection, was a curious mix. He played games with the other children, on the manhole covers and round the lamp posts of the street where he lived. On weekday evenings after school they would all be out, between the dismal, brick-built terraces of Rushden, with the clang and smoke and dirt of a newly industrialised town around them.

Then at weekends and in the holidays he lived a different life. He would be wheeled in a wheelbarrow to his grandfather's plot on summer mornings, to spend the day working the land and listening and 'pretending not to listen' to the gypsies and the rivermen and the other smallholders, until 'the accent and look and feeling and colour of country people and things' were pressed on his mind 'with imperishable indelibility'.

Or he was taken for longer walks by his father, crossing the county border into the Bedfordshire woods, woods that 'etched' themselves on his childish mind, 'with such imperishable clarity that I can still see and smell the bluebells, the honeysuckle . . . the sheer concentrated fragrance of summer leaf and sap.'

If the countryside was what pressed itself indelibly, 'etched' itself on his mind (they are both visual arts metaphors), still the town was where he lived. As a result he grew up with both influences held side by side and in balance. Added to which, he had chapel and school and his father's severe Methodism in one ear and he had the woods and fields and his grandfather's heresies in the other. And as he grew, so the contradictory influences multiplied and increased.

At sixteen, unable to afford to take up his place at Cambridge, Bates was working in a shoe factory warehouse. All day, when he wasn't either cleaning the outside privy or making inventories of 'bags of grindings, sprigs, nails, rivets . . . and sacks of powdered glue', he was reading Chekov and Turgenev and writing his first novel, until he got the sack. At night he walked miles alone, looking in at lighted windows and making stories. Prisoned in work and desperate, he came to hate the Midlands, the flat and sullen fields, the 'scabby, jumped-up, chapel-cum-villa towns' of his childhood. He married his Rushden sweetheart and together they left and chose Kent instead, for its softness, for its folds, for its great wooded rounds.

So Kent is where the wood of *Through the Woods* is still to be found, just below the village of Little Chart Forstal. It lies in the angle of a lane running down from Bates' house, ankle deep in sweet chestnut litter and with its main path still closed for the preservation of the pheasant and its trees on the far side still contemplating their reflections in the waters of a stream.

Looking back at it coming into leaf at the end of the first chapter, 'There is something about it,' he says 'that makes it the best wood I know.' But then he corrects himself. It is only 'almost the best wood. For me, there is one better, though I never go to it now.'

The best wood is in the rejected Midlands, a wood that as a child Bates would be taken over the border into Bedfordshire to visit, a day's excursion in a pony and trap. It was the first wood he knew, 'a paradise of a million primroses' and at other times of the year full of nightingales, butterfly orchids and the 'little fiery scarlet hearts' of wild strawberries. Characteristically it was a wood below a railway cutting, so already compromised and contradictory. Through it, every five minutes the sound of the train would smash, 'a strange exhilarating sound, a mad roar . . . echoing against a thousand branches.'

After the train, in reward, there would be a silence that was all the more intense for the interruption, 'unearthly in its quietness'. And this is why it is the better of the two woods. It isn't just the quiet that is unearthly; it is the whole wood, reconstructed as it is from memory, a hundred miles or more and a childhood away. Here something important and unseen was at work. Wandering alone away from the safety of his uncle's garden, the six-year-old Bates would surrender to the powerful spirit of the wood. It was a 'dark and in some way exhilarating drug' whose effect was hypnotic, and which he says he craved. He talks of being put into a dream and on coming out again, of a spell being broken. 'To a child,' he says as he closes the chapter, a wood has something about it 'that is not quite real. It belongs very nearly to the world of mystery.'

Like all paradises this one is lost. As he says, 'I never go there now.' Part of the reason for this is that the woods of childhood no longer exist. Even if it hadn't been grubbed up in favour of the logistics parks so beloved of the Midlands, returning as an adult would mean looking at it with different eyes. So it is lost temporally and geographically, because he grew up and left childhood, because he chose Kent over the Midlands. And it is lost most of all because it was never fully grasped.

There is a ghost that haunts these woods where we first feel fear and temptation in equal measure. Flickering at us between the trees, it is 'the distillation of another and more lovely world', somewhere just over there, that existed either in a time before, or not at all, but that we sense, or imagine, or see gestured in the world of the wood, but that is inaccessible to us and therefore permanently lost.

Bates lived through a time of extraordinary change. 'In the early thirties,' he points out, 'not a single farm worker in my village had a car, many not even a bicycle.' By the seventies even cottages would have four or five cars and the village shop that used to sell string and boiled sweets and paraffin and fat bacon had a freezer 'dispensing scampi, smoked salmon, spaghetti bolognese and exotics of every kind.'

Growing up almost under the skin of the land, as he did part of the time, with the rest spent in the town, often with his head in a book, Bates couldn't help asking himself continually what to do with man in the landscape. Is he master or creature, creator or destroyer? Is there some way that he could or should be, or is it all hopeless? In fact, nothing in his writing is ever hopeless. Pop Larkin's philosophy, 'the need to go with the stream, never to battle against it', is also by his own admission Bates'. He can write in *Down the River*, the companion volume to *Through the Woods*, of the 'privilege' of taking part 'in every act which went towards making the bread I ate.' With nostalgia he can list the procedures, many of which were lost or replaced in his own life time, the drilling, hoeing, rolling, sheaving, binding, shocking, carrying, stacking, threshing, sacking, milling, running for the yeast, before he could taste the bread, 'sweet, dark . . . very nearly the colour of the earth which had grown it.' But he can also argue for the increased mechanisation of the countryside, for improved communications, for better wages and living conditions for the rural poor, for the closer communion of town and country and even for the birth of the 'town countryman', increasingly the only countryman left to us now only half a century or so later.

Acceptance of what look like irreconcilable differences is something that Bates absorbed from his own upbringing and from the natural world that lay about him, very early on. It deeply characterises his writing. The destruction of Chelveston woods to make a disastrous airstrip in the Second World War is 'ruthless murder' but it is also, and in preface, 'necessary'. That is not to say he doesn't have preferences, or state them openly. In fact he is frank about them. He would cheerfully change the 'near useless wonders', the jets and televisions and space craft of the modern world, for the bloodshot eye of his old uncle and the smell of woodsmoke and the woodland flowers.

Every so often another anthology of 'Nature writing' is produced, and Bates is pretty much guaranteed to have a chapter or two to himself. He wasn't really a Nature writer. He was what might be called a Natural writer. He was a novelist whose craft was learnt through rigorous effort and through reading but whose perceptions are like those of the birds and animals he describes, quick, innate and part of a habit, as it is described in the *Autobiography*, of 'thinking through the pores of my skin'. His observations are natural in the strictest sense. They are not those of an outsider with a notebook, who conscientiously records the appearance of bud and leaf and flower. They are those of someone who belongs. He doesn't need to record detail. He knows it.

Similarly his habits of writing are natural in more than their subject matter. They instinctively reflect the nature of the English landscape and its climate. It is easy to overlook how embedded his writing is in the landscape that produced it. Bates' starting point, often stated, is that man, while being responsible largely, if not in some places entirely, for the form that the landscape has taken, is also inalienably *of* it.

What John Berger was later to call the landscape's 'address', Bates takes as a given. That is, in Berger's words, 'the way a landscape's character determines the imagination of those born there.' So, for Bates, born within reach of a river valley, 'not in it, nor above it' but able as he put it, to stand 'on flat but raised ground' and to look across and around on all sides, the result was, that 'we saw things squarely, at a proper distance, on a proper plane, in a proper perspective. And that gave us perhaps, in that district, the sturdy independence for which we were noted.'

The landscape is in part its people and vice versa. Bates is always sharply observant of locality. On the particular character of the Midlands, he notes that it is 'a county of ugly and bastard speech, of stout independence, of stone and pasture.' Here the people and their character and the shape of the land they inhabit and the way that they speak, are all jumbled together as though none were more significant than any other, as though all were perfectly valid ways of describing a particular place.

When describing the Kentish woods for instance, Bates doesn't hesitate to use language imported from the Midlands if he needs it. Sheep pens in winter are 'dreary with sludder'. Pheasants fly away with 'flacking wings'. It is obvious in both cases what he means but a flacker in particular is a very precise Northants word. It is a piece of card pushed into the spokes of a bicycle wheel to make a noise. Even lulled among the chestnut woods of Kent 'the ripe, rough, Midland vernacular' comes to his mind because it is part of him. His connection with the landscape, both past and present, is lively, naturally complex in the truest sense.

And England is a complex place. It is small. Its fields and hedges and stone walls and woods are all man-made, so it can't help but absorb and reflect human emotion and endeavour. Its climate is fickle, its tricks of light always referring back or forward to other times. It is deeply and essentially nostalgic. Unashamed and old-fashioned nostalgia is one of the most noticeable features of Bates' writing, to the modern reader, and this too is a reflection – a reflection both of what he sees before him and of what he feels within, of a mood shared between them, bred as he is out of the landscape he describes.

Towards the end of *Through the Woods* there is a long passage called 'Winter Spring'. It is an intense evocation of light imprisoned in raindrops on a dull day. 'This extraordinary stillness and suspense creates a strange feeling of melancholy. Much has been written of the joy of spring, but very little of its melancholy. Yet the earliest sense of spring, coming with the first light cold evenings of February, or with the weak sunlight of flowerless January afternoons or with those periods of mild suspense in December, is filled with an indefinable sadness. It is one of the oddest and sometimes one of the most charming characteristics of English weather that at times one season borrows complete days from another . . . And it may be that these milky days of winter, which seem borrowed from April, are automatically filled with the sadness of things out of their time.' It is as though the landscape too has a memory, can spend days out of season lost in its own dreams of renewal.

We have a horror of nostalgia now. We think it better conscientiously to concentrate on the concrete rather than the emotional or the purely aesthetic, to talk about working the land, to exhume vocabularies that refer to dead skills, wooding or peat cutting or drowning of water meadows, as if the knowledge of these things will somehow jump-start our connection with the lost landscape. But if we called nostalgia, 'home-sickness' which is what it really is (*nostos*, a return home; *algos*, pain or grief) would we be less ashamed to confess to it? Home is where we grew up and where we belong. Home is what produces us. It is ourselves in the end. It may be that nostalgia over landscape is healthier than its opposite.

In an essay called 'Overture to Summer', Bates goes even further. Considering the part that weeds and wild flowers play in the lives of men and animals he reaches the conclusion that life without weeds would be 'economically and aesthetically' poorer, 'perhaps even dislocated'. Nowadays 'dislocation' is something of a buzz-word. Finding it in writing of the 1930s and '40s is strangely disorienting. It has the dizzy feel of anachronism. We use it now to mean separation from place but what it most commonly means is to put out of joint, to dislocate a limb from the body it belongs to. And that is how close Bates means us to understand man's connection with the landscape to be. Without recognising our position in the landscape, without reaching an accommodation with it at its fullest and most diverse, we will become like disjointed limbs, sick and useless.

It is a position he shares with W. H. Hudson, a writer he particularly admired. There is a brief tribute to him in Bates' *Autobiography*, at the end of which Bates includes a quotation from Hudson himself, a passage that Bates describes as 'Biblical'. It goes like this, 'The blue sky, the brown soil beneath, the grass, the trees, the animals, the wind, the rain, and stars are never strange to me; for I am in, and of, and am one with them; and my flesh and the soil are one, and the heat in my blood and in the sunshine are one, and the winds and the tempests and the passions are one.'

But if Bates is nostalgic he is also robust. There is nothing pious or mealy-mouthed about his ability to embrace the nature of the world. He enjoys its contradictions. He never pulls his punches about his own background for instance. 'Plebeian by birth and upbringing' as he calls himself, he says he has a 'habit of looking at things in a cockeyed way.' He upholds poaching. He condemns hunting unless the fox be substituted for a 'milk-maddened cow'. He hates gamekeepers and one in particular 'with a good, simple, hot-blooded hatred.' There are good things about the town and there are bad things about the country and if life is impossibly mixed and various, still it is all one and you are part of it, joined to it as closely as a limb is joined to a body. It is possible to dislike your knees or your ankles but you have in the end to accept that they are your own.

Nostalgia for the worlds that are lost is always balanced by optimism. Bates was actively interested in progress and reform. He tried, as he put it, 'to look at the country as a whole, as an inseparable part of the whole English way of life, and not as a life separated and fenced off.' He believed in agriculture as something 'creative' and beneficial, especially to 'millions who never take part in it.' He was robustly optimistic in the face of change, even when those changes were mourned by him for their private preciousness. Our affections are linked 'to the little things', he wrote. 'Are they merely the tender trivialities of one man's recollection or are they eternal things?' And in poignant reply to his own question, 'Don't ask me,' he says, 'They are very dear to me and I am frightened of the answer.' It is a characteristically clear-eyed perception.

So it is alright to be nostalgic. It is just not alright to hold on, to decry change, because change is in the nature of things. And in the end, if all the 'tender trivialities' go and we are really homeless then at least there will be the woods and fields of memory. And maybe these fusions of the real and the ideal are where we really keep our selves. Maybe this consummation of contradictions is at the heart of it, however fleeting. So standing in his wood at bud-break, in the rain, Bates describes the rain intensifying the colour of the buds and the buds colouring the rain, until the separate identities of the two seem confused, subsumed as they are in some newer and bigger unity. He watches while 'the whole woodside gleams with the liquid passionate glow of multitudinous rain-drenched branches' until the buds 'become glorified'. It is what he would have called a 'Biblical' passage, light and water and wood transfigured in 'passionate' combination.

Only in memory or on paper can these fleeting things, tricks of light, days out of season, lost traditions of work or play, lost places, the woods full of orchids, the 'paradises of primroses' be fixed. But it is these intangibles that are powerful to us, the world of mystery for the child in the train-shaken wood, the memories of the man of another county, the illusion or promise of something better, different, more permanent, that keep us going.

This is what writing can do. It can make of these complex and impossible things, something coherent, something fixed that is solid enough to nurse and uphold us whatever we have lost or destroyed. It can give us a place we can walk into at the author's invitation, a place where there will be 'all kinds of trees, all kinds of flowers and creatures, a conflicting and yet harmonious pooling of life.' A wood.

That is Bates' answer to his own question. This is what 'the English woodland' is, a triumphant amalgam of real with ideal, the solid with the evanescent, the presence of Kent and the memory of Bedfordshire, described in the language of Northamptonshire. It is a collection of lives, imagined, remembered and real, all coexisting, each separate and distinct and often warring, sometimes killing or crowding, but that put all together, pool into one. Variety and conflict mysteriously producing harmony.

Abstracted like that, it makes a pretty good recipe for society as a whole. The perfect illusory paradise of our dreams. But it could just as well be a recipe for Bates himself, for his strong and contradictory character and for the writing to which he dedicated his life and which so closely reflected not just his own nature but the nature of the landscape that he loved. Deceptively effortless, literary and earthy, imaginary and intently observed, painterly and full of sound. Real, ideal, optimistic, nostalgic. Accepting of the way things are.

Or just natural.

Laura Beatty
Salcey Forest, 2011

THE WOOD IN APRIL

THE WOOD IS NOT FAR FROM THE HOUSE. You can see it, in fact,
from the windows. We might as well go straight down to it.

It is one of those early April mornings that are neither warm nor
cold and the light on the land is a kind of spring half-light, not shadow
and not sun, a soft and rather treacherous glimmering from behind
the north-west cloud. The wind is quite strong and in open places
finger-cold, and there is a continuous dancing everywhere of branch
and flower and even grass. On the open green outside the house there
is only a row of elms and chestnuts to break the wind, and the trees
are still not in leaf. So the wind comes straight across, rippling the
pond into a little sea, with dark fitful little waves that must be quite
stormy for the moorhens. The grass on the green is a thin speary grass,
grown tussocky, and the rains of winter have flattened it into a kind
of brownish-yellow mattress. It hardly moves in the wind. Above it,

however, many lady's smocks, standing in small mauve companies, dance and fret incessantly. There are no other flowers, except an odd dandelion or two and some patches of celandine almost hidden by grass, and except for them and the yellow fluttering of distant daffodils through garden fences, it might still be winter.

But we turn right from the house, going south-east, and instantly it is better. And after a few moments, when we are off the green and into the lane itself, between the thick high hedges of haw and maple and holly, it is infinitely better, another world. The lane is cut deeply out of the earth, the banks rising up from it sheer for three or four feet, so that later, when the hedge is full grown and in full leaf, it will be like walking in a roofless tunnel. Even now, the difference is wonderful. The wind does not trouble us at all. It makes an incessant swishing in the pines overhead and in the hedge tops, a whining, melancholy noise, and yet in some way sweet. But below, in the lane, the calm is quite miraculous. We walk in stillness, in a primrose world of absolute spring.

We can see the wood quite clearly now. It runs along a right angle bend of the road, so that we look at it broadside on. It looks quite small and yet, for some reason, very solid, as though it stretches a long way back. Actually it is not very large. Far behind it, and high up, on the face and crest of the downs, is a wood that is large. It spreads like some colossal wild black rug over the back of the down, so that for three miles at least no earth at all is visible: nothing but this monumental mass of trees, an immense and almost primevally magnificent wood that is a landmark for a dozen miles. Beside it the wood in the lane looks no more than a spinney, a neat domestic little copse. But from a distance, as I say, even from a short distance, it gives the impression of solidity, of endurance, of having been there a long time. From our angle also it seems to be composed of a single species of tree. It seems to be a solid mass of white birch trunks.

They are breaking into leaf at last. They are losing, for the first time
for nearly six months, their look of sombre ruddiness, as though
their branches had been dipped in burgundy. And if there were still
any doubt about spring it is dispelled by the birches: the green of
their leaves has that infinite tenderness that it will never have again
all summer. And there is not yet too much of it. The green leaves are
merely like so many soft paint splashes among the dark branches.

So, from this angle, the wood looks not only solid, but awake. It is
almost the best time to come to it; the between time, half bud, half
leaf. The leaves will never show up again with the same brilliance,
except in autumn. And there is something else that will never show
up again until autumn, as it shows up now: the big spread of bracken
that is really the beginning of the wood. It begins at the very angle of
the road and comes down to the edge of it, bordered by a hawthorn
hedge that is so thin that it is not really a hedge at all. This bracken
is dead and it has been dead for six months. There are no trees on it
except some misshapen gorse bushes, some odd oaks and two sallow
trees, now green with catkins that are past their best. So the bracken

stretches openly for about fifty yards until there comes a point at which it fuses with the wood. It is in reality a point of overlapping, birches overlapping bracken, bracken running under the birches, the trees at first thin and small, then gradually thicker and taller, until they annihilate the bracken and rise in a solid mass of white trunks that are brilliant in their own shadows. I have described this bracken because, though it stands dead and dry and ready for the complete annihilation by its own new leaves, it stands as a perfect foil for the wood. Its pale fox-colour shows up the trees in a wonderful way. The trees look supremely rich against its dry deadness. They are thick and sweet with the life the bracken has lost. Even so the bracken is not so dead as it looks. It holds another life, a little paradise of small bird life. In unthinkable spots, in mere tangles of dead bracken twisted by rain and wind and frost, it houses nests too cunning for even boys to find – little miracles of moss and feather built invisibly into precarious clumps of bracken stalk, the work of tits and robins and wrens, nests only found by chance or great patience or by the accidental rousing of the birds themselves.

There is a path through the bracken, but it is accidental. Presumably one must not use it. I will say why in a minute. I do use it. The real path, the path through the wood, lies lower down the road. It goes through the heart of the birches, a wide bracken-flanked track that switchbacks up and down and is cut by deep tracks of timber wagons that have been fetching out the sweet chestnut thinnings during the winter. After about fifty yards it splits. The timber track goes straight on and the public path veers to the left and goes downhill. It is at this point, standing on the crest of the hill and with the paths branching, that you see the wood at its very best. You are standing in the heart of it. It lies all about you – not a big wood, not grand or primeval or overpowering at all. Yet it seems big. Its boundaries are invisible. The birches close in thickly behind you, shutting out the road except for a yard or two. Before you, along the flat and down the slope, the big oaks and sweet chestnuts and the few distant pines and wych elms thicken just enough to shut out the river and its meadows and, in summer, the sky. The sounds of the outside world are dimmed, gone. The wood echoes with sounds peculiar to itself: the furtive treading of pheasants among the big papery chestnut leaves, the clap of pigeon wings, the squawk of blackbirds, the sound of rabbits scuttling to hiding, of jays laughing. The wood magnifies them all, gives them a certain quality of excitement, almost of mystery. They in turn magnify the silence, which is itself mysterious, an expansive hush without wind, the strange silence of a small and confined world.

We take the downward path. At the crest foxgloves are thick, but flowerless yet of course, all over the place. Among them and beyond them, and in fact over every inch of wood, as far as and even beyond its boundaries, the bluebells are also thickening for flower, a million spikes with dark hearts of bud and here and there a breaking out of petals. They cover the rich sodgy wood soil like shining green reeds, everywhere.

Among them and perhaps because of them there are few primroses, fewer anemones. The bluebells crowd out everything, drown the whole wood floor with great pools of flower until the trees, in May, seem to be standing in deep lakes of liquid mauve.

But now, in April, the wood is not rich in flower. Chance bunches of primroses, a white scattering of anemones, a few almost transparent cups of wood sorrel: nothing more. It is not even very rich in leaf. The sunlight comes down into it unbroken except for a mere netting of shadow. The hazels, catkinless now, have scarcely begun to break, the oaks are brown and bare, the chestnuts have only prim buttonholes of leaf. The honeysuckles alone are green, bright scarves of green thrown over what seem beside them the drab hazels.

We go down the slope, quite steeply. The path is wide, there is a sense of spaciousness. Formerly hazels and young Spanish chestnuts overgrew the path, but a winter's thinning has opened out the whole wood, the old high trees alone remaining. The thinning has, in fact, been a revelation. Hidden trees have come to light. For the first time for years some great birches stand visible, surprisingly white, tall as oaks. We shall see, in May, the whole sweep of bluebells.

But the river still lies invisible and, for those coming for the first time, unsuspected. It is the bridge that finally gives it away, a small white bridge running from wood to meadow over what is, really, in spite of the maps, no more than a brook. It is not more than ten feet wide and, in most places, not more than one foot deep. It flows very fast, between steep banks, jingling and diddling and rippling over a bed of sand and stone, the water clear as wine, the water weeds spun out by everlasting water motion into very long emerald skeins, yellow water lilies thick in summer in the odd three-foot pools, yellow mimulus, the monkey musk, dipping down almost into the water on the woodside. In summer, moorhens sail and paddle away in fringes of meadowsweet and burnet and loosestrife that enrich

the banks far beyond the wood with cream and wine, and in hot weather snakes swim above the trout like fish themselves, big silvery worms shining in the tree-darkened water.

This fusion of wood and water is an entrancing thing. Without the wood the stream would be nothing: a mere thin watercourse winding through its flat meadows. Without the water the wood, on its slope and with its air of quietness and mystery and of being a world within itself, could not help being a constantly delightful thing. But water and wood, together, shading and watering and bounding each other, each give to the other something which the other does not possess, the wood giving to the stream something solid and shadowy and immemorial, the stream giving to the wood all the incomparable movement and twinkling transience of moving water, the tree shadows standing deep in the stream, the reflection of sunlight flickering a kind of waterlight up into the shadowy branches of pine and alder. The wood and the water are here, in fact, one, for each other and with each other. It is a fusion that is almost perfect.

There is, to my mind, a single imperfection, a solitary snag. Here one must go back. There is no wood beyond the stream. There is only an immense view of the ridge of down, with the great wood like a black skin thrown over it. And between it and the little stream there is only a stretch of arable and pasture land, of prim fields with stocky thorn hedges and many sheep. It seems better to go back.

But to go back means, of course, to go back through the wood – legitimately, the same way, by the same path. And always, doing that, I feel a sense of anticlimax. It is better to go back illegitimately, to trespass. By doing that we can skirt the wood on its south side and come out finally by the keeper's hut, through the path in the bracken.

Under the wood, on the south side, it is suddenly quite hot. The sun is coming out a little and there is no wind at all. We are shut in by woods. They make a solid rectangle about the field, shutting out completely the wind and the world. All these are separate woods, intersected by paths and in some cases by dykes, and they are all good woods to look at, thick and solid and with the last burnings of sallow and hazel flower still smouldering along their boundaries. But beyond that they hold nothing. Inside they are dark and in some way dead, the undergrowth a brutish tangle, the wet spots stinking with garlic. There are woods that have no spirit of life at all, that are not worth entering. And these are like that.

So we go straight on, under the almost sultry woodside, until the corner comes, the turn, the angle of the wood beyond which the bracken begins. The keeper's hut is in sight. We have almost completed the circuit. Between two young oaks, on a stretched string, hang the keeper's victims, the wild enemies of the precious tame pheasants whose destiny in life it is to be cared for more tenderly than most babies and to be massacred a little more brutally than most soldiers. There they hang, the enemies of the squirearchy: half a dozen hedgehogs, a brown owl or two, stoats and weasels, jays and magpies, a whole fur shop of young grey squirrels, with one almost white, a pure silvery grey that should have made a good cheap fur for any keeper's wife. And here, too, you see the reason for much of the wood's quietness, its lack of apparent life. Its life is systematically exterminated: all life, that is, except the pheasant and the rabbit, who are reserved for death on a socially higher plane. For the heart and core of these woods is contained, for those who own them, in one small space, a little oval: the pheasant's egg. If you do not understand this, if it seems to you extraordinary or fantastic or even monstrous that the egg of one bird can create a position of autocracy, let me leave you here, so that you may moon about the wood to your heart's content until, some time between now and five o'clock, the keeper comes. You may then discover a curious thing: that for him, the keeper, you are no more than a snake or a weasel or a hedgehog, a predatory beast, a potential sucker of tame eggs. To him you are just that. It will not avail you anything at all if you tell him that you are interested in natural life, that you have never touched an egg in all your born days and that you are there solely to taste the wood and the beauty of the wood alone. You are regarded by him as a potential poacher, in spite of all your protestations of innocence and in spite of the fact that you may not know a snare from a potato net or even, just as likely, a rabbit from a hare. It does not matter. The pheasant is the lord of life, the almost divine sovereign of the woods. You must not, by word or look or trespass, do anything to upset his chances of ordained death. Like the murderer who falls sick on the eve of execution, he must be kept alive, tenderly, jealously, at all costs, in order that the state, the squire, may not be cheated of the ultimate satisfaction of prearranged extermination.

There are those who talk of the evil spirit of woods. But for me there is only one evil spirit of woods: the keeper. I suppose that, somewhere, there must be keepers who are pleasant, considerate, friendly men who love their wives and smile and exhibit other signs of common humanity. But it has never been my luck to meet one. Keepers are, I feel, brutalised by the life they lead: the double-dealing life of servitude and autocracy, by the constant ironic necessity of having to preserve to kill and to kill in order to preserve. It is not their fault; they are victims of a system of organised sadism; and very likely, I think, they never understand it. So they are men with more enemies even than a rat, with many many more enemies than the poacher they hunt. They are hated everywhere. It is a hatred in which I join. And in which I am unlucky. For it would be just my luck if, at this moment, just as we were almost out of the wood, the keeper were to appear. I might quarrel with him as bitterly as I quarrelled with that other keeper, the young man, with the sunburnt, queer, brutal stare, of whom I shall have much more to say later. Now I will only say that, quite avowedly and quite simply, I hate him, with a good, simple, hot-blooded hatred, and that no doubt he, in turn, after four years, still hates me.

But luckily our keeper does not appear. We walk across the bracken and under the few oaks and sallows and so out to the road. The sun is shining a little, but the wind is still cool, and the dead oak leaves rattle in the wind. And standing on the road we can look back. In a break of sunlight the wood is suddenly lit up. It is a mass of burning branches, of buds about to break into the first flame of summer.

It looks extraordinarily beautiful. There is something about it, in fact, that makes it the best wood I know.

THE OTHER WOOD

I SHOULD SAY ALMOST THE BEST. For me there is one better, though I never go to it now.

I was born and brought up in a woodless country, almost a treeless country. To the north of us we had a wide river valley that was, I think, without even a spinney. To the west of us we had other towns as treeless as our own. To the east, three or four miles off, we had half a dozen copses, the remains of what was once a great wood, and two or three fox coverts of larch, planted by landowners. It was not until we got far out to the south and south-east, a distance of six or seven miles, that we got to country that could be called wooded, a country of immense estates and immense mansions, where the ridings of the woods were kept almost as neat as suburban lawns. In relation to that country we spoke of going to the woods.

It is, today, an absurdly modest excursion: a journey, by car or bus, of ten minutes or so. Twenty years ago it was an excursion into another world, a colossal adventure. It was never undertaken lightly. It needed much preparation. It took time. It took us the better part of a morning to get there, what with the stops at this pub and that garden fence, and the stops to let the horse wind and make water or the stops to let him drink water and make wind, and it took us, for the same reasons, the better part of an evening to get back. We never went for less than a day and we were lucky if we went more than twice a year. We talked about it for a long time before we went and for longer still when we got back. That journey to the woods was, in fact, as important to us as a Cabinet crisis or a coronation. It was undertaken with all the forethought and seriousness of an expedition. We prepared ourselves against the possibilities of storm and drought and starvation. We might, in fact, have been going for a year and a thousand miles, instead of a stone's throw and a day.

Actually there was not the slightest need for these industrious preparations against famine, since we were going to relations who in the first place had been forewarned of our coming and who in the second place would have exactly the same fears for our starvation as we had ourselves. Nor should we go thirsty. For we were, in fact, going to the house of my Uncle Silas.

I have been debating with myself whether or not, at this stage in my life as a writer, it should be necessary for me to explain my Uncle Silas. His notoriety has extended so far beyond my control and my anticipation that, sometimes, I feel disinclined to acknowledge his creation. Actually, in fact, I did not create him at all. He existed. He was the living flesh-and-blood brother-in-law of my maternal grandmother and, among other things, the biggest reprobate who ever lived. It is not, happily or unhappily, my privilege to have created him, any more than it was Dickens' privilege to have created

Micawber. The best characters in fiction are almost invariably lifted straight out of life. I did that with Silas.

Even so, there will be readers of this book who have never met him. For them I will only say that he was a short, almost dwarfish man with a devilish face made doubly devilish by one bloodshot eye, that he was extremely ugly, as cunning as a wagonload of monkeys and as wicked as sin itself. He drank too much and, as I have explained elsewhere, he never washed himself. Such delicacy and decency was for him altogether a waste of time, and the women of the house washed him instead. He was very old and, in contrast to the wine of which he drank so much, the older he got the worse he got. At the age of seventy-five he had undergone a serious operation on, I think, the bladder. He was six weeks in hospital. It might at least have impeded him, if not killed him. Actually it seemed to rejuvenate him, and he went gaily on to live another fifteen years of aggravated wickedness and cunning. Age meant nothing to him. Time merely ripened him. He was, indeed, almost too ripe. The history of my Uncle Silas, plainly told, on paper, would be one with Sterne and Rabelais, and this, in any case, is not the place for it. One of the greatest of his few virtues was that he was a marvellous gardener. He grew things that no one else did and grew them better, bigger, earlier and more cunningly. If you could get round or over or under Silas, as a gardener, you could beat the Devil himself. His small garden lay under the shelter of a wood. It was that wood to which we made our excursions and that wood which was for us the whole symbol of the journey.

It was, above all, the first wood I ever knew. It was a paradise of a million primroses. They crowded everywhere, often attracting many small birds about them, all through the wood and outside of it, very big and rich in that black earth. We took baskets to gather them and with them many big white violets and countless rosy-white anemones. And later in the year came the bluebells, and later still, in the first weeks of June, the moon daisies that were like milk all along the woodside, and the meadowsweet, like the cream of summer. The wood stretched from the very door of the house to the very brink of a railway cutting and every five minutes or so the woods were shattered by the sound of passing trains – a strange exhilarating sound, a mad roar of sound smashing and echoing against a thousand branches.

After it the wood seemed unearthly in its quietness, the potter of
rabbits almost comically soft, the scream of a blackbird no more
than the squeak of a toy doll. Later still in the year we came to that
wood for wild strawberries. I see them now, as I have not seen them
since: little fiery scarlet hearts in the summer-scorched leaves, sweet
as sugar. And then later still, but more rarely, we came for nuts. But
somehow, by then, the best of the year and the very best of the wood
had gone – primroses and orchis and moon daisies and strawberries
and even the birds. There were no nests. The nightingales had long
since been silent. Only the garden was rich, almost exotic, with fruit
and flower: black elderberries wine-rich on the woodside, yellow
apples falling, great scarlet dahlias shining like dying suns against
the dark trees. If it rained, as it often did, we could only sit in the
house and listen to my Uncle Silas telling some devilish tale that was
probably all lies and gaze at his vast collection of birds' eggs hung
about the walls on long strings, like strange heathen necklaces. If
it were fine we talked and walked in the garden. In autumn no one
wanted the woods and I walked in them alone.

They seemed then, and still seem, of great height and expanse. They
spread all about me, for miles and miles, shutting out the sky, the
house, the railway cutting, the blaze of dahlias, the whole world. They
stood about me with uncanny silence broken only by the late moan of
pigeons, the passage of invisible tiny feet on the already falling leaves,
and that regular five-minute smashing past of the trains. They were
a world in themselves, a world that to a child was slightly forbidding
and discomforting, the smell of them alone tranquillising, the old soft
sweetness of wood-earth, mustily sweet, the immemorial distilling of
uncountable flowers and leaves, the odour that only comes from the
timeless decay under trees in almost sunless places, the black scent of
ceaseless growing and dying and fermentation. It was a smell that in
spring I did not notice. It was there, but the sweetness of primrose

and bluebell somehow changed or effaced it. But in autumn, at the damp turn of the year, it was powerful, everywhere. It was almost the wood itself, a dark and in some way exhilarating drug that was its very spirit. And like a drug it led me on and on, in a craving to drink it more often and more deeply. That scent of woods is indeed almost hypnotic. It puts one into a dream, a dream in which as a child I walked along the soft dark silent wood path as far as I dare and then reluctantly and dreamily back again, until the passionate blaze of dahlias or the sound of Silas's devilish voice or the smell of woodsmoke broke the spell at last.

It broke: but not completely and not forever. It remains. If I shut my eyes it returns: the evocation of a whole wood, a whole world of wood-darkness and flowers and birds and late summer silence, of a million leaves turning mellowly to death. It becomes then more than the mere memory of a wood, the first and the best wood I have ever known. It is the redistillation of another and more lovely world.

TREES IN FLOWER

AND HERE, SUDDENLY, a hundred miles and twenty years away from it, there is a change even while one is looking back. It is almost May, and suddenly on a late April morning the wind changes, north to west and west to south, and the sky is softened into a sea of white islands, the sun breaks hot, and the wood, as though reflecting that warmth and that whiteness, breaks suddenly into columns of shining smoke. The wild cherry is in bloom.

For about four months, from March until the end of June, the wild flowering trees of this country are at their best. Unlike the trees of gardens, they seem to have no years of shyness, the uncertainties of cold and rain and sunshine never seem to affect them, and with one or two distinguished exceptions they flower only at that time, between first spring and midsummer. Yet while they flower they are immeasurably glorious. The best of them are the trees of poets; they are to the world of trees what the lily and the daffodil are to the world of flowers. The humblest of them are the treasure grounds of bees, the ivy in late summer as rich with bloom and honey-scent as the sloe is thick with scentless stars of snow in March. And all are common trees, hedgeside and wayside trees for the most part, with nothing exclusive or niggardly or exotic about them. They are the friendliest and loveliest of trees. The blackthorn opens the season and the honeysuckle, I suppose, ends it. And they stand distant not only in time but in almost all other respects, in scent and shape and colour and effect, the blackthorn so very cold and snowy, the little star-shaped blossoms so pure and icy, the real pristine emblems of the breaking spring, and then the honeysuckle rich and sun-coloured, the flower head a lovely and fantastic clustering of many flowers in one, a cornucopia of softest amber and cream and ruby, with the scent of heaven. And if the blackthorn is one of the shortest and perhaps even the very shortest of all in its season of flowering, then the honeysuckle is certainly the longest. It begins in midsummer and goes on through haytime and harvest, renewing itself in warm autumns until that richness of wine and amber is lost among the colours of dying leaves about the empty cornfields. The Irish, I think it is, have a legend that the honeysuckle is the strongest of trees. They might with equal truth have had a legend that it was the tree that never rested. For the flowers have scarcely been replaced by the shining cherry-coloured seeds before the vine is breaking into new leaf again, so that often in midwinter the honeysuckle is the true evergreen of the woods, in brilliant and almost full leaf long before the black branches of the sloe have been threaded by the flower buds of cream that are its first signs of life in March.

The blackthorn blooms on into April, reaching its glory as the cherry begins. By the end of the month the cherry out-flowers it. There is something earthy about the blackthorn; it is a dwarfish tree, almost stunted, always near the earth. But the wild cherry flowers against sky, in white grace and magnificence, with true

ethereal loveliness, visible from afar. In orchards the cherry will grow to great extent, but not height. But in woods the wild cherry, hemmed in by oaks and chestnuts and trees of equal growth, rarely grows to great extent, but very often to immense height. A wild cherry will grow to seventy feet, flowerless until the extreme tip lifts itself above the crowd of neighbouring trees, the thick white clustering of blossom floating above the wood like a cloud on the mountain of colouring branches, never still in an April wind. After the catkins, it is the first glory of the woods. It is equalled only by the hawthorn, the may, the first glory of the hedges. The may is erratic; of all the wild flowering trees it fluctuates most with the season. The cherry blooms infallibly in April, but the coming of the may is never certain. Often on May Day it would be hard to find the traditional branch of it, though I have seen it in bloom in other and colder springs in the first weeks of April. But when it finally blossoms there is no uncertainty at all about it; its flowers are the risen cream of all the milkiness of May. Its scent has the exotic heaviness of summer in it, very like the pungent vanilla half-sweetness of meadowsweet. It is so like the blackthorn and yet so unlike it; the blackthorn, with its black naked twigs that have no suppleness or tenderness, bears flowers of frost, but the may branches are never cold or stiff or naked. The leaves of emerald are full blown and the flowers with their pin-hearts of claret spill and foam and cascade down the hedgesides with a summery richness that no other English tree, not even the elder, can equal, splashing the grass and the earth underneath them with cream that turns to pink as time goes on and the sun increases.

The crab comes with the may, and the elder after them. The crab stands apart. It is the sweetest of all trees, the pure cups of pink and white truly sweet, without the vanilla drowsiness of the rest, the upturned blossoms smooth and light and shining, like spring silk. And after it the elder, bringing back the odours of may and meadowsweet again, only half-sweet, falls again like the may in great cascades of even richer cream.

How is it that this current of cream and white and pink goes on and on through the wild trees of England almost without break or variation? The chestnut and the crab and the wild rose and even the blackberry are white and pink. The dogwood and the elder and the lime are cream. The rest are white. And all are scented, either with that summery faintness of the may or with the absolutely pure sweetness of the crab and the

chestnut and the rose. We have no wild exotic blossoming trees of scarlet or blue or purple. There is a sort of northern delicacy, almost fragility, about them all. The flames of the chestnut candelabra burn sweetly and quietly, many little flames of softest pink in the white cups of wax above the drooping clusters of seven leaves. The rose has no passion, only that immeasurable and matchless sweetness that fills the hot days of June and July as the heavenliness of the lime drenches the summer nights.

Gorse and broom alone break the sequence of pink and cream and white. And curiously they are the smallest and most brilliant of all. They are trees of flame, the broom flaming up in May with little passionate tongues of yellow, the gorse burning throughout the year from one end to another, flickering or flaming up with solitary or countless flames of blossom according to the season, never resting or going out, a tree of perpetual flowering fire and darkness.

FLOWERS AND FOXES

A<small>ND NOW</small>, with the cherry in full blossom, the primroses at their fullest floppy lushness and the faint dark smoke of bluebells obscuring and finally putting out the fritillary lamps of the anemones, there is no longer any doubt about the wood or the spring. They have become synonymous, full of tree blossom and ground blossom and the ceaseless passion and passage of birds. The wood is alive as it never will be again. It is still a month from the edge of summer, trees are still more branch than leaf and all day long the birds have no interval of silence at all. And if the fullest frenzy of song, with nightingales and blackbirds mad in the drowsy hay-noons of June, has not been reached, there is a clarity and a shouting of bird life everywhere that is like a silver mocking of winter. The wood is full of it. The trees, just full enough in leaf to form a light sound canopy, seem to take the sound of singing and fluting and pinking and scissoring and throw it down the aisles and ridings until it is

magnified through a new crescendo into a new beauty. One thrush
fills the whole wood with a clash and jingle of silver. One pigeon
moans and moans it into an almost summer slumber. A solitary
cuckoo beats it with a bold and endless double note into an echoing
monotony. The wood now is never silent. There is a constant mad
rushing of blackbirds, low and fierce in flight, from place to place
among the hazels, a sudden spring laughing of woodpeckers in the
treetops. Noons are as noisy as mornings, evenings even fuller of
clamour than afternoons. That summer break for silence, the hot
bird-stifled uncanny emptiness of June and July, is a long way off.
There is an everlasting restlessness everywhere.

When there is no singing or flight or nest building there are
passionate interludes of mating: the fierce pursuit of blackbirds,
the fickle beckoning and twittering of chaffinches, hen dancing and
simpering from many cocks, cocks fighting, the chosen mate taking
his fierce little thrill at last, a rosy-breasted gladiator taking his spring
prize. And along the ridings the cock pheasants strut like warriors,
painted cheek and jowl, arrogant and scarlet and bold with the
mating fearlessness, the hens quiet and invisible somewhere among
the bluebell-pierced blanket of sweet chestnut leaves, nesting close,
so close and toning so miraculously with that silvery brownness
of leaves that they escape, sometimes, even the eyes of keepers,
miracle enough in itself. You come upon them, quite often, in bold
and unexpected places, almost stepping on either hen or eggs, the
eggs having that same silvery brownness as the back feathers. It
is only the lightning flick of the black-brown eye that betrays a
sitting pheasant: the sudden blink and the swift nipping cock-up of
the head, only momentary and down in a flash, but somehow too
quick and electric for the stir of a leaf. And even then, found, she
will still sit there, tight and fearless, feathers down-smoothed, eyes
still, head ruckled down into the crinkled cringing neck, still sitting

there and still sitting until something, when it seems that she never will move, startles her at last into crazy and ridiculous flight and the revelation of the nest and its almost hot eggs.

They are, now, almost the only eggs in the wood. Pigeons will build in the birches, later. Kingfishers and moorhens nest with regularity just beyond the wood edge, in the bank of the river. There is report of a woodcock and there are a few odd blackbirds and thrushes in the chestnut stumps and faggot dumps left by the woodcutters. But this whole wood, six or seven acres of it, like so many other woods, can show only a tenth part of the nest life of the open hedges in the lane. No chaffinches, no tits, no linnets, no wagtails – a strange emptiness, as though the wood were too big for such small creatures or too sunless or too dangerous.

It must be dangerous. The predatory population of a wood is very great. Filled with all sorts of egg suckers, stoats and weasels and hedgehogs and magpies and jays and the now terrorising grey squirrel, it can only be an enemy country for the small bird. In that sense the wood is disappointing. It is quiet and secluded, shut off from wind and hail and not yet quite shut off from the sun, and it ought to be a paradise of nests. It never is. I have hardly ever known a wood that is. The struggle for life in a wood seems too fierce and too great. Its nocturnal conflicts are endless, altogether too powerful for the hopes of birds no bigger than a child's hand.

But if there is no paradise of nests there is, just now, at the lower end of the wood, on a stretch of marshy ground dotted about with big sallows, a paradise of flowers. All along the course of running and seeping water that trickles down through the wood to the river itself, there is a blaze of kingcups. They grow in immense luminous islands, gigantic buttercups among lush clusters of pink-stemmed burnished leaves of bottle-green. From a distance, from the rise of the wood, they shine as nothing else ever shines in this wood until the scarlet fungi, like Russian cakes, blaze in scores under the autumn birches. And now, in their full glory, they stand like water torches in and about the oozing, trickling water, pure gold, clear and brilliant and more burning than any noon. And all about them, softer, altogether less gaudy and pristine, the most modest of flowers, perfectly contrasted with them in form and colour and effect and everything: many, many lady's smocks, the milkmaids of children, blowing softly everywhere like stems of mauve smoke. If the kingcups are lamps, the lady's smocks seem only like lamps gone out, little candelabra extinguished into a smoke of flowers.

Everywhere too the leaves of wild iris sword up strongly through black earth and water and the ferny leaves of meadowsweet. In late May and early June the irises will begin a blooming that, later, will fuse into and be finally hidden by the meadowsweet: the carrying on of a long lineage of yellow, burning out, growing infinitely more tender, by some process of inversion, as the year goes on, until the final yellowing of frost, most delicate of all. It is as if the kingcups had lit a far too passionate flame for the rest to follow. The wild iris, blooming in high summer, should reach the crest of colour, should be a sun-passionate torch, since it is so shaped, growing defiantly, drawing its flame as though by some contradictory miracle from the water at its feet. Instead it is an altogether modest flame, a little deeper than lemon, unfurling from leaves that are appropriately soft, smooth swords of olive that will twirl in the little waterside breezes in sudden starts of motion, making a sound like the flapping together of a loose flag in a summer wind.

But these irises and these summer winds seem still a great way off. Only the lamps of the kingcups and the extinguished lamps of the lady's smocks burn now in the open clearing of marsh. Red orchises are coming out among the unbudding bluebells – or rather they are not red, but a pinkish magenta, varying a great deal in colour, as

they do in size. They are the kingfingers of children. So what with kingfingers and kingcups and kingfishers and lady's smocks, the wood in May has its own royalty.

It is, in fact, a royal place for children. To them it must seem an immense kingdom, the boundaries of which they can never quite grasp. Its trees are almost supernaturally vast; even the hazels are great. To a child there must be something about it all that is not quite real. It belongs very nearly to the world of mystery. A field can be seen and understood and explored. Whereas in a wood the wood is very much hidden by the trees: there are countless darknesses, unknown places. It is an exploration into the unknown. It is at once a joyful and fearful place. Children are never frightened in fields, except by cows or by the hostile appearance of irate hats. But they are very often frightened in woods: by the very mystery and seclusion of the place, by the sudden soft hushings of leaves, by the magnified echoes of feet, by the leaping up of rabbits, by the savage sudden screechings of unknown birds.

They are things which, in broad daylight, mean nothing to us. But night changes them, or it changes us. A wood at night, or even more at twilight, can be a strange place. Fear begins to come more quickly in a wood, with darkness and twilight, than in any other place I know. I have been in a wood gathering violets or orchis or primroses in the late evening, when the sudden realisation of twilight coming down has sent a sudden damnable running of cold up my spine, and I have half run out of the place. That feeling is common. The path through this wood of ours in the lane is public; it leads from one village to another. It is used a good deal by day. But there is precious little use of it by night, except by the local poacher. People will not use it. 'Damned if I'm much on that old wood at night. Lumme if I ain't glad when I get out of that place.'

What is it? Why is it? It is not simply darkness. We grow used to darkness. It can only be some quality in trees themselves. They impinge on us, hypnotise us more or less by the new fantastic shape that darkness has given them. At one period of my life I did much walking by night: long vigorous walks out of the town into the surrounding country. It was a country that was almost treeless, but if I walked far enough I reached woods. Reaching them, I at once used to turn back. They had some powerful quality of darkness, some awful intimidating blackness that I could not face. I have been in woods too by day when I have been glad to get out of them again, to see the sky. It may indeed be that shutting out of the sky that feeds fear. There is an extraordinary comfort in the sight of the sky, of clouds and sun by day, of starlight especially by night. Space and distance kill fear at once. It nourishes on littleness and confinement, and it is in the little spaces under the confined branches of woods that it flourishes at times almost into terror.

But if I have sometimes been glad to leave a wood by day I have oftener been sorry. I sat once in a wood on the north border of Bedfordshire, in April, by a keeper's hut, eating an orange. It was perfect weather, quiet and sunny, with a little wind blowing about the hazels. I had walked up the wood, along still ridings, seeing more primroses and also more oxlips, which are like wild polyanthus, than I had ever seen before or in fact than I have ever seen since. By the keeper's hut there was a biggish pool. Very still, overshadowed by trees, it looked like a stretch of black glass. All over the place was a windy clapping and brushing of bare ash and hazel and, every time the wind turned, a great breath of primrose scent.

Suddenly there was an unexpected stirring about the pool: a flicker of brown, almost fawn, and then another and another. The first I took for a rabbit. Even about the second I had some doubt. After the third and fourth and fifth I had no doubt: they were young fox cubs. They came tumbling up out of the holes in the pond bank, in and out, up and down, rolling over and over, playing an endless game of chivvy with each other, until I could count thirteen. As a boy, I once held a lion cub in my hands: he was fawny-gold and like plush, a wonderfully soft golden cat with a sleepy blinking face. Those fox cubs playing in the woods were very like him: so many little fawny-gold cats playing with a kind of pretty devilry up and down the banks of the pool, running out into the primroses, doubling back, rolling each other over, their light fur all the time ruffled and rosetted by the light wind, until they seemed like the prettiest creatures in the world. I sat there for a long time, watching them. The wind was just right, blowing from them to me, and they never suspected my presence. They were endlessly fascinating, tireless in their own devilries, lovely with their sun-coloured fawn and their grace of movement up and down that steep bank, on the edge of the water. And finally I had only

myself to blame for upsetting it all. Not satisfied, I moved nearer, slowly and, as I thought, quite soundlessly. Getting much nearer, I stood still. I could see them better. They had still no suspicion of me. Then, in a moment, I moved on again. I made no sound, but in a second they were all arrested, electrically, in alarm. They stopped for a single second, cocked their heads and gave one look at me. In another moment they had gone tumbling down like golden balls into the dark fox holes, out of sight. And I have never, by some damnable chance, seen a fox cub since.

OAKS AND NIGHTINGALES

SUDDENLY, about the middle of May, the white flowers of the cherry are gone and, in their place, all over the wood there is a great upclouding of yellow, not bright yellow, like a field of mustard, but a greenish yellow, a kind of lemon olive, very beautiful and at first, in the May sunlight, quite startling. It is the oaks in flower.

Until now the oaks have been obscured, principally by birches, now light emerald, on the upper side of the wood, and by the alders and pines on the lower, by the waterside. They form, with the Spanish chestnuts, the heart of the wood. It is they who create, from June until September, the almost sunless summer darkness, the intense leaf-shadow that can be almost cold in a hot noon. As oaks go, they are not old trees: two hundred years perhaps. They have a girth just about like that of a pillar box: they stand stoutly, in their prime, and, since they have been grown quite close, very straight. Even so, they have stood there obscure, leather-budded, decorated high up with their few wintry apples, strung on the boughs like the big wooden beads of some native islander. Now suddenly they have undergone this magnificent rejuvenation, an abrupt vivid change from leather-brown to olive-yellow, from obscurity to flower. They light up the whole roof of the wood. Rising above the birches, they become the upper sunlit edges of a great cloud of leaf. And on these shadowy sunny days of May the light does sudden tricks with them, catches a solitary one in a cloud shadow and ejects it again, so that the one tree burns up briefly like a vast candle of yellow; or it catches half the wood in light and half in shadow, so that when the wind moves the cloud again the shadow rolls away like smoke, light tumbling into shadow and the broken shadow finally into unbroken light, into a great sun-stilled balloon of honey-coloured leaf.

So, collectively, from a distance, the oaks look magnificent. They are really kingly now, not only leafed, but pinked with new apples and tasselled with their innumerable little hanging flowers, very delicate, almost too delicate for trees of such girth and ruggedness. This contrast and combination of strength and delicacy gives the oak a rare quality; it makes it, in May at least, supreme among the trees of the wood. It is undeniably supreme here because this wood of ours contains neither beech nor ash, though there are sapling ashes on the south side, nor sycamore nor maple, both trees very beautiful in bud, with their creamy wine-coloured or rosy Japanese buds breaking into curious Japanese leaf.

The perfect wood would have these trees, and larch as well, more Japanese than ever with its drooping pin-fingers of bright emerald and its scarlet knots of flower. It ought also to have hornbeam and whitebeam: but more of them later. It might well have some chance bird-sowing of wild laburnum, as there is in a Midland copse I know, where two great light-strangled trees hang their flowers just clear of the tallest hazels, a flaunting yellow, showing just how yellow yellow can be, turning the surrounding oaks almost pallid.

It is in fact only from beneath the oaks, catching their olive against a deep May sky, that you can see their real vividness. The same holds good for ashes and beeches. You must get under them, lie under them, and look up. The brilliant light comes down through leaves that are still thin-skinned and delicate. They let the light right through, so that they seem, as you look upwards, to be almost transparent, to be made, the beech especially, of some shining leaf celluloid. They seem to intensify, at the same time, the blue of the sky, to clarify and deepen it to a faultless turquoise. It is a perfect combination. Moreover, the chance of it never comes again all summer. It is only in May that you can lie or stand or sit in a wood and see that intense lofty miracle of light and leaf, the off-setting of green by blue, of leaf by sky. In another month the sky will be shut out. There will be a sky of leaves in its place.

It will be a sky, also, of one colour: the almost uniform dark green of high summer. Beech and oak and birch and chestnut and sycamore will seem, in July, like the same trees. Now, in May, it seems incredible that summer and the sun can burn them into that uniformity. They flame now with such individuality of colour, with all the greens under the sun, that it seems impossible for anything to change them.

It seems as if the beech can never become anything but emerald, the oak olive, nor any of them any different from the colour they

hold so gloriously, as if permanently, in May. And since now, also,
bluebell and campion and orchis are in full bloom, blue and pink
everywhere, there is no doubt that the wood looks at its best.

It also sounds at its best. Cuckoo and blackbird and nightingale,
by the middle of May, are calling together, the blackbird all day long
and in spite of everything, the cuckoo and nightingale passionate in
the warm spells, shy and almost silent at the slightest turn to cold and
wet. The cuckoo mocks everything in the too bright early mornings
and is himself mocked into silence before noon by wind and cloud.

He goes with the weather like a cock on a church. He is all a clatter of arrogance in sunshine, charming us to death, monotonously cuckooing us into wishing him silent. Then suddenly he shuts up, vanishes. All through the spell of cold and wet we hear him from some mysterious distance, as though he had found, somewhere, an inch of summer for himself.

The nightingale is also fickle, but on a different plane. He seems amazingly temperamental. Far up in the thickening oaks, nothing but a slim bud himself, he is hard to see; also, like the cuckoo, he often vanishes completely, effaced by wind and wet into silence. But when he sings, at last, there is no mistaking it. There is a notion that, since he is so named, he sings only by night. It is quite mistaken. He sings all day and, at the height of passion, all night.

It is a strange performance, the nightingale's. It has some kind of electric, suspended quality that has a far deeper beauty than the most passionate of its sweetness. It is a performance made up, very often, more of silence than of utterance. The very silences have a kind of passion in them, a sense of breathlessness and restraint, of restraint about to be magically broken. It can be curiously seductive and maddening, the song beginning very often by a sudden low chucking, a kind of plucking of strings, a sort of tuning up, then flaring out in a moment into a crescendo of fire and honey and then, abruptly, cut off again in the very middle of the phrase. And then comes that long, suspended wait for the phrase to be taken up again, the breathless hushed interval that is so beautiful. And often, when it is taken up again, it is not that same phrase at all, but something utterly different, a high sweet whistling prolonged and prolonged for the sheer joy of it, or another trill, or the chuck-chucking beginning all over again. It seems to be done out of a kind of devilishness, or in a kind of dream, between intervals of sleep, as though the bird begins its phrase and drops off and then, waking again, takes up what it thinks it remembers.

The nightingale is not common here. We hear it, but never with that consistent multitudinous performance that, in some woods, keeps people awake at night. I am in fact surprised that we should hear it at all, here in a wood whose most constant music, winter and summer, is the keeper's shotgun. I am surprised that it does not shatter that tiny bud of a bird into a far greater silence than even the longest of its own enigmatical pauses of passion between phrase and phrase.

THE VILLAIN

THE KEEPER IS NOW, in fact, more than at any other time, the villain of the piece. You must not step an inch away from the path; you must not look at a pheasant's egg; you must not gather a bluebell. In fact you must not do anything, by word or look or deed, even in innocence, to upset the course of the drama in which he is a star performer. The pheasant and its egg have become sacred emblems; the wood is a hallowed and forbidden place.

The position of the keeper is an ironical one, a paradox, though I doubt if he would know it. He is at once killer and preserver, at once guardian and thief. He cannot help this; it is his job and he is the victim of another law as inexorable as his own. He is the paid accessary after the fact; and, like many accessaries, paid or otherwise, he often displays, consciously or unconsciously, a more singular brutality or meanness or enthusiasm than those for whom he acts. It is a remarkable thing that, if you approach the squire or the landowner himself with some request for permission to walk here or there, the result is almost invariably courtesy and decency, even in refusal. The same, generally, with the bailiff. If you are lucky, it may be almost the same, though never quite, with the head keeper. It is when you reach the lowest points of the scale and make contact with the hands of those who, by necessity, do the dirty work, that things are changed. It is like the old fable of the ass with a little authority, except that it is not a fable any longer, but a reality. The dirty work, the brutality, can be delegated and delegated so far but no further, and there comes a point at which the onus of it, however dirty and however brutal, must fall on somebody. It falls, of course, on the accessary after the fact, on the hireling, on the under keeper. And since the dirty work is mainly a process of killing and bullying and pursuit, for the ultimate result of which someone higher in the scale gets all the credit, there is bound in the very nature of things to be refining of the lower instincts and an obliteration of the higher. In short, somebody, somewhere, some way or another, is going to be brutalised.

It may be that I am prejudiced against keepers; that, having sprung from a people brought up to hate them, I have inherited that hatred myself. It may be that I am simply tactless and unlucky. It may be, also, that a keeper, if an evil at all, is a very necessary evil – the human element that is essential to keep the scales of nature balanced. I don't know. I only know that it is my experience never to have met a really likeable keeper and that it is my unshaken conviction that a life of killing to preserve and of preserving to kill must, sooner or later, in some way or another, brutalise those who lead it.

We were living one year, my wife and I, newly married, not very far from the old home of my Uncle Silas. On a cold May afternoon, miserable with icy rain, we went out, muffled in overcoats, to look for nests. It was a vile day and we should never have gone. But under the shelter of the wood, in the hollow, it was just tolerable. We went across two fields and then came back.

Coming back, I observed a figure behind a hedge. I have an innate suspicion of figures behind hedges. They have a powerful suggestion, whether still or agitated, of hostility. And it was clear, even from a distance, that this one was hostile. But we kept straight on, as though nothing had happened, until we came to the point where we had to pass it. Some time before that point I saw the barrel of a gun.

Suddenly we drew level and the keeper had his moment: the moment of little authority, of bullying power, for which the underling lives. He challenged us:

'You know you're trespassing?'

'No,' I said. And thought: 'Nor do I care a damn.'

'There's no footpath here! You get off, quick.'

I forget what I said. It was four years ago. It may be that I was not polite, that I made an unguarded utterance. I forget. But suddenly his face was lashed into livid temper. At best it was an ugly face, not ugly so much by its natural lines as by the marks of life on it. It had been brutalised. It was a villainous face, at once strong and stupid. Coloured dark red by temper it was revolting.

'You get off this land! And stop off! There's the footpath over there. You get on it and stop on it.'

There followed a slight altercation. It was not polite. My wife walked on. There was some brandishing of musketry behind the hedge and, on my part, some deliberate perverseness and some unfeigned anger. A tactful person would not have done this. There would have been a standing of drinks, an offering of cigarettes. Unfortunately I do not smoke and I have not yet come down to standing drinks for keepers. It was tactless, but there it is. I made an enemy. My consolation is that we were enemies, constitutionally, before we met.

That was the beginning. It is a drama in three acts. Nothing happened

for many months. I forget how many, but it was still summer when, one evening, I was coming up from the river on that same path, though half a mile away. The river, at that point, was a beautiful piece of water. Narrow and shallow and winking everlastingly on its bed of stones it came along under a copse of chestnut and alder, through small bridges of stone under which trout moved darkly, and between an endless double embroidery of willowherb, loosestrife and meadowsweet, a long edging of pink and cream flower lace.

I had been watching the trout. Then, going on, I saw the keeper. He was coming down the path. I could have turned, have gone back or sidewards, along the river; I could have got out of it gracefully. I went straight on.

When we met, this second time, we were saved the necessity of any introductory formalities. Having met, we were free to behave with good, honest, bare hostility. We did. Again I forget what we said: only that this time, since we were alone, we were saved the tiresome necessity of veiled politeness. It was a swift, hot performance. He kept asking me over and over again why it was that, since I knew I was trespassing and had been clearly told not to trespass, I still continued to trespass. I ought to have replied to that, and I see it now, with extreme coolness, ironically, almost off hand. Instead I shouted: 'By God, if I told you you wouldn't understand! You're so damned big and silly.'

He dropped the bucket he was carrying. Bucket in one hand, gun in the other, dog at heels, he had been from the first formidable. He would weigh, perhaps, thirteen stone: somewhere very near the heavyweight class. I myself weigh a little over ten, just above the lightweights. One sock under the jaw, at that moment, could have landed me, temporarily, beyond the reach and care of temporal things. And it looked for the moment as if I should get it. Bucketless and gunless, looking powerfully villainous, he stood squared to fight. It was a delicate situation. I did not know what to do. One hit, and I was in next week. Unconsciously I did the very best thing. I stood still, making no movement at all. He stood in turn like some irate batsman waiting for the ball. Quite clearly I was the ball, but gradually, since I never came on, he began to look, and no doubt feel, a little ridiculous. His pose became purely symbolic. Gradually it ceased to be aggressive, even dangerous. It ceased, finally, to mean anything at all. He dropped his hands.

I am not saying that this was, at all, a glorious victory for me. It was only that, by refusing to be put out, I had not been put out. I was agreeably astonished. But what astonished me most was that the whole show was dangerously charged with hatred and malice, with a spirit of ugly brutality that I had never met before. Having been brought up in a town notorious for its poachers, I had heard something of the eternal hostility between poachers and keepers, but I had never met it. It had always seemed to me that it might be a case of fifty-fifty. But the poachers I had met had, though cunning and remorseless, never been brutal or brutalised. They were adventurers in necessity, victims of a paradox also – the last hunters in England who were also hunted. Their craft was never vicious. Yet here was someone, a young man, who was both so brutalised and vicious that he resembled the traditional warder of the American film, a man brutalised by the brutalising of others, an ugly sadist, a man driven by hatred into hatred until he lived for nothing but hatred

and the pure malevolent pleasure of it.

I may have overdrawn this comparison, but it will hold good. Hatred and the effects of hatred had left their marks clearly in a face that, even at best, could never have had too many softening features. It was not only a physically ugly face, but a spiritually ugly face. In anger it turned the dark-blooded, almost purple, colour of bad meat.

It is a considered simile, perfectly apt. The warder comparison also came to be apt, later.

It was autumn, and on a dark mizzling evening we had gone to gather mushrooms in the fields beyond the wood. It was warm and still everywhere, perfect mushroom weather, the whole countryside mild and dripping with the rain mist of September. Going down, we heard shots in the wood and I hoped it was some saucy poacher, out in the half-light. The mushrooms glowed everywhere in the summer-burnt grass like knobs of silk, and we slushed about in high boots and piled up the basket, alone in the dreamy wet landscape that

smelled of rain and wet earth and the first turning leaves and mushrooms.

Then my wife said: 'Don't look. He's coming.' I knew at once who she meant, and I looked up to see him come striding from the wood, face darkening, gun under arm. As he came on I circled off, stooping and picking and going on. He circled with me. I came back. He turned. I pretended not to see at all. Until finally we came within speaking distance.

'You bought this land, now?' he shouted.

'Is it yours to sell?' I said.

He came on, with the old habitual hot-tempered malevolence I now knew very well. He shouted something about being hard up for sixpence and I retorted, I forget what. It must have been something a little provocative, because next moment he was up with me and had hold of the basket.

My wife, who had hitherto shouted encouragement in remarks like 'Take no notice', 'Ignore him', 'Who is he, anyway?' now came on too, and she also caught hold of the basket. That was responsible for a remarkable thing: an act approaching politeness on the part of a man already furious with rage. He let go the basket. Feeling morally justified, I flared up. Who the hell was he? What game was he playing? Hadn't he any manners before a lady? 'Take no notice,' my wife said.

He also spoke. 'Get out this field,' he said. 'Get out!'

It was then that he became exactly like the warder. For, gun in hand, he proceeded to march us, ignominiously, out of the field. We walked, all the time, ten or twelve yards ahead of him. It was just near enough for us to carry on a conversation of ironical asides just loud enough for him to hear. It was about the time of the Hitler massacres. 'Hitler,' I said, 'would be glad of him. A nice man with a nice gun like that.' We raised our voices just enough. 'He's too big for Hitler,' my wife said. 'Much too big and much too good looking.' It all enraged him furiously: we could feel the rage in the air, in the way he followed us, relentlessly, to the gate.

At the gate he had, in fact, almost caught up with us. It was there that we had a great chance. By the time we had opened the gate he was ready also to come through. Very carefully we slammed it in his face.

It was as though it had hit him. He tore it open and came after us. I fully expected, at any moment, a kind of comi-tragic charge in the backside. We had still another field to go. He had fifteen acres, roughly, in which to shoot us and we did not improve the situation by a continuance of ironic asides, kept up until we reached the gate leading to the road and beyond which we should be free. And all the time he came on, like a warder conducting us in or out of exile. Then, at the second gate, we had the second chance. It was exactly like the first. By the time we had opened the gate he was ready also to come through. But he had not the brains to see it. Very carefully, with this time a kind of sweet deliberation, we slammed it again into his face.

I never saw him again. But I hate one keeper as much as another; and I have gone into it all solely for one purpose: to show why even at home here, in May, with the wood at its loveliest, with the bluebells like blue flower pools under the flowering oaks and the nightingales passionate in the oaks themselves, we take the trouble to seek fresh woods.

WOODS AND HILLS

THERE IS NO BETTER PLACE for seeking fresh woods than the hills. The hills lie to the north-east of us, in what seems to be a single straight-topped mass of woodland, beneath which immense scars in the chalk shine out like snow. On days of good visibility, of that treacherous too-good visibility which can only mean rain, they stand out with uncanny clarity, wonderfully detailed and near. And then on dull days, on summer mornings of heat or mist or on vaporous soft evenings, they seem very far away, and consequently gigantic. Those mists give them distance and turn them into mountains, into gloomy masses of earth lying beyond the vast plain of a continent. So transformed, they are hardly recognisable. They seem foreign to us and to the very English, very homely valley beneath them. And again, on early spring days, in March or February, before there is any colour of leaves, they will turn bright blue, a half smoky, half sea-coloured blue, beautiful and arresting, almost unearthly, as though the woods had turned into a forest of blue branches. And in dead of winter they will seem to stand there with an extraordinary savage solitude, with the woods all along them looking like the wild black pelt of a beast thrown raggedly over them. They respond to the strangest and abruptest terms of season and light, never the same from one day to another, never dull, always surprising: gloomy and brilliant and blue and copper and wild and soft by turns.

And now, on the first real clear hot days of May, they share with other woods the thousand-coloured pattern of new leaf, distance turning whole trees to mere stitches of jade and copper and emerald and olive and white, a vast spring-crazy fabric without design. But even from a distance its colour and texture are very different from the colour and texture of the wood here in the lane. The scale is altogether vaster, the trees more varied. The wild cherries stand like great hill pagodas of white. The spruces are vast tents of emerald. It is distance not only lending enchantment but rarifying it, heightening it, not tricking it into a false loveliness but giving as it were a new telescopic view of the loveliness existing in actuality.

Because, happily, it is not only an enchantment of distance. It persists and increases right up to and into and through and beyond the woods themselves. In landscapes seen from afar off it sometimes happens that what are seen as dolls' houses of pink and blue sugar turn out, when seen more closely, to be only very undoll-like and very unsugary bungalows. But here, with the hills, that does not happen. There is a change, but only of angle. There is no disappointment, no sense of cheating. The cherries are still cherries, the spruces still spruces. They seem, if anything, more beautiful.

The road comes up very steeply from the lower land. Narrow, almost a gorge between its high banks crowned with the crimson and cream of dogwood and viburnum, it is almost always a dazzling white, fiercely and dustily white in the May sun. And as you go up it you see, at its best, the outer magnificence of the wood. It has ceased now to be a spring frolic of crazy leaves. It towers up like some immense tree fortress, a hundred and fifty feet in height, a towering architecture of branches that sweeps right up and over the great crest of the hill. From below, from the tiny white road, it looks perhaps greater and higher than it really is. It can only be the effect of the hill.

Such a wood, seen on the level, would seem only like a palisade of trees, straight as a fence. Here, because of the round rise of the hill, it is not only the sides of the wood that are visible, but the top, the whole roof of it. It is like some paradoxical bird's-eye view seen from the bottom of a hollow.

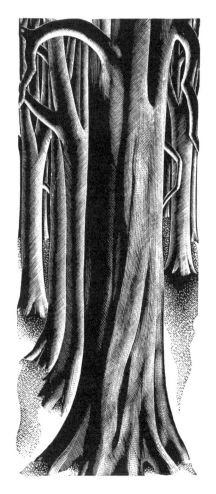

Thus you can pick out the trees, the new and almost strange trees that are foreign to the valley. There are trees that appear, even from so close, to be smothered in slender caps of dusty-bloomed white blossom. They have the appearance of dim magnolias. They are hornbeams, which seem to have sucked up the chalk into leaves that are like flowers themselves. They grow randomly, all about, lighting up the black of the wood with their striking magnolia candles. Larch and pine and a few birches, with many cherries, crowd among them, but, as far as I remember, no oaks at all. They have no place on the chalk, and they seem in some way foreign to hills. Similarly there are no sweet chestnuts, only a few horse chestnuts, flaming pink and white among their flopping umbrella canopies of green.

It is the beeches that are the undeniable glory of the hills. They have been grown here very closely, so that they stand on either side of the deep-cut tracks like vast pillars in a church of trees, straight as pines, extending far up and down the hillside in steep grey aisles that create an effect of massive and incalculable solemnity. They are literally grand; they give out grandeur, a grandeur of strength and almost awful nobility. Beneath them the wood floor is clear except for odd yews and hollies, which in turn only heighten the effect of that unadorned magnificence of naked trunks rising up and blotting out the sky.

You can walk under that vast roof of beech boughs for hours, for half a day, without retracing your steps, without turning back on your tracks at all. It makes the small wood in the lane seem a plaything of a place, a mere handful of birch and oak, a child's bouquet of trees. It has, for me at any rate, a powerfully silencing effect, an effect of paralysing elation. I prefer to go to it alone, not to wander in it for the mere sake of solitude, hands uplifted in a praise of ecstasy like some lorn female, but because that effect of elation is an effect almost of stupefaction. I cannot think. I go on in a dumb wandering walk of staring and listening. It is the beeches that do it. Up at the north end of the wood, where the beeches lessen and give way to a run of hazels and, now that I come to think of it, a few oaks also, the tension at once lessens, and I feel a sense almost of relief and escape. This change of trees means a change also in other things. Under the beeches almost the only flowers are the slender aristocratic helleborines, little orchids of pale cream that come up through the illimitable depth of light beech mould. Unspectacular but aristocratically lovely, they hold the dark wood floor almost alone. Whereas, higher up, among the hazels, there is a perfect madness of flowers: bluebell and pink orchis, forget-me-not and campion and willowherb, with all the late summer ramping of coarse gold and white. It seems as if the beeches are somehow omnipotent, as if they suck up all of life from below and blot it out from above, leaving nothing. Under them there is always that sombre and almost awful stillness, scentless and colourless except for the smell and eternal copper of dead leaves, the unflowered floor stretching away as far as they stretch and breaking only when they break.

Here the flowers break above them in quite a madness of bloom, and also below. All along the sun-scorched chalk, under the lowest of the beeches and beams, there is an endless golden coinage of rock roses. They go on all summer, little gnarled knotty bushes trailing all over the chalk, each flat lemon blossom lasting its one day and giving place to another. That effect of yellow against white, of flower against chalk, is dazzling. The rock roses dominate the outer edge of the wood as, far back, the beeches dominate the heart of it. Among them and with them go sprinklings of harebell and, earlier, cowslip and, more seldom, orchids of rare kinds. The fringe of the wood is in fact a crazy pattern of unexpected things. Scarlet eyes of wild strawberries wink out of sun-parched grass, leaves of geranium out-crimson their flowers, big silk-shelled snails lie on the path like the chocolate striped eggs of some nestless bird, clematis fluffs and balloons like caught wool from among the bloody tangle of haw and rose. The rock roses and the chalk alone weave their unchanged thread of gold and white, breaking only at the roads and the many tracks that cut into the wood and split it across like scarring veins.

The best of these tracks, the greatest, which runs all along the ridge, under the vast beeches, like an arid vein of chalk and leaf

dust, is something more than a track. It is a piece of English history, the track made immortal by the passage of devotional feet, by the sweaty journeys of countless pilgrims, Chaucer's among them: the Pilgrim's Way. And if this road needed any other monument than *The Tales* it has it here, in its immense cathedral canopy of beeches. They shelter and dignify it and, in a way, keep it secret, preserved for the very few pilgrims who still care to track along it, in the cool summer shadow and silence of trees, while the traffic for Canterbury and Margate and the sea roars over the hillside a mile away.

I come down from the hills, always, with marvelling reluctance, constantly looking back. There is something about hills that performs a miracle of change on woods. The trees grow vaster, higher. What explains it? Up there, in the fields beneath the wood, the soil is like salt, like the salt bed of a washed away sea. There is no nature in it. The whole white stretch of it, with harrows putting up dust-clouds over it like cannon puffs, looks heartbreaking land. Crops are starved; yet trees grow as though there were an unfathomable richness of soil, into a new hill of wood rising out of and far above the hill of chalk. The really rich soil of the valley cannot show a dozen trees like the thousands of these beeches. They defeat reason. They are a monumental paradox of richness from poverty.

I take my last look back at them from the garden gate. A mere segment between cottage roofs is visible. In bright sunlight it takes on its old look of a piece of fabric, with its white and emerald and olive stitches of leaves. Distance gives it a delicacy that, within the wood itself, is never suspected. And somehow it seems perhaps too delicate. It has the impermanence of spring. And if I stand and take an extra long look at it, running my eyes over its soft-coloured patternlessness, it is not out of mere daydreaming, but because I know that in another month, or less, it will be changed out of all belief.

THE HEIGHT OF SUMMER

BY JUNE THAT CHANGE HAS COME: not merely on the hills, but on the hedges, in copses, through the woods, everywhere. The land is caught up, almost completely, in the green vortex of midsummer.

It happens suddenly, almost imperceptibly, before one is ready for it. The horse chestnuts are alight and out again, standing dark above great rings of shed petals; the wild cherry vanishes suddenly into obscurity, the crab with it; the oaks are flowerless. The canopy of leaves in the wood becomes stitched closer and closer until, by the middle of June, it is like a tent roof, dark green, shutting out the light. Foxglove and the first willowherb are in bloom now, scarcely distinguishable at a distance, growing together in erect close masses of pale strawberry colour; bracken fronds are unfurling faster than beans, curling up out of their own dead leaves and among gorse and broom and over the faded bluebell spikes like many pale green shepherd hooks, to be forged gradually by the heat of the sun into a stiff straightness. There is a first lighting up of wild roses on the wood edge, pink and white, and of purple orchis and butterfly orchis, in the coolest places under the trees. In the marshy spots wild iris burn dreamy yellow torches, their leaves twiddling and flapping almost soundlessly and almost ceaselessly in the small summer winds.

The butterfly orchis are not rare, but they are not common. They look rare, almost ghostly on their straight green stems, whitish-green ghost butterflies that are scarcely visible in the bush underwood. They have a rare other-worldly scent, exotic, almost oriental, a little sickening. One becomes aware of them more by scent than sight.

For me they are reminders of great occasions, of drowsy midsummer afternoons when we walked, in order to visit my aunt at her pub in Bedfordshire, through the wood where they grew and where, I hope, they still grow. That wood, a small square wood remarkable only for one other thing, was drenched with the exotic, almost tropical scent of hundreds of those ghostly orchis. Often, merely passing through, we never saw them; we only caught that wonderful sweet-drugging scent that was somehow ghostly too, rich but pale, overpowering but elusive. They are, for me, the strangest of English wildflowers. They seem in some way foreign. They stand like pale green spirits, almost unreal.

Apart from them, the wood is remarkable for this. It divided, for me, one world from another. Up to its boundary extended my known world. Through it and beyond it was another country, unknown and spacious, a wide green world the heart of which was the small white spot of my aunt's pub. That spot was invisible until we were through the wood. Once through the wood we could stand on a high clear ground and look down, over the hedgeless acres of corn, and see that spot, lying like some pure white heifer in the green fields beyond the church.

It must be forty years since my aunt began to keep that pub, and only five or six years since she ceased to be the landlady of it. It is, and has been for all my lifetime and probably hers too, a small, very low-roofed pub with a thick crust of dark bird's nest coloured thatch, whitewashed walls, and long rather prim bow windows in the early Victorian manner. The sign, *The Chequers*, is set at the top of a white pole, which rises in summer from a lake of marigolds in the garden at the front of the house. The Bedfordshire fields slope upwards on all sides, straight from the pub doors, so that the place looks more squat than perhaps it really is. On the stream that flows past the garden railings there is a perpetual procession of white and brown ducks, which waddle about also among the hens in the pub yard; so that the garden paths, the thresholds and the yard itself are covered with hen and duck droppings and little convoys of white and brown and red feathers that float and bounce against the earth like angels of fresh thistledown.

Like the pub, my aunt does not seem to have changed at all in my lifetime. I see her dressed in perpetual black: not the black of crêpe or mourning, but a kind of rook's black, shining and silken, the black of authority and austerity. She is a sturdy, stocky woman, with a face of apple red intersected by many little veins of darker red and purple. She seems to be forever frowning in reprimand. In reality she is smiling, not so much with her mouth, as with her eyes. They are bright grey eyes and are framed in an infinite network of little creases and wrinkles. And she cannot keep her mouth still. It twitches. It is as though she would like to laugh but will not, as though she has schooled herself, as the landlady, not to make a public exhibition even of an emotion like laughter.

I do not know which was best known, my aunt or the pub. Very likely they were synonymous and so reflected each other's reputations. Certainly the pub reflected the character of my aunt. It was not prim, and I am pretty sure it was not always proper, but it had about it a

kind of austere homeliness. The floors were of polished brick, the tables were scrubbed like bleached bones, and the lamps shone like altar brasses. There were three rooms, the bar, the smoke room, and the parlour, and they had characters of their own. And just as I see my aunt in perpetual black, so I never think of the pub without remembering the mild beery smell that all her scrubbing could never wash away, the odour of lamp oil and the faint fragrance of old geraniums sun-warmed in the summer windows.

It has always been a modest and dignified little pub, of a better class than an alehouse, and yet never in danger of being mistaken for a hotel. Occasionally, in the shooting season, my aunt let rooms; in the summer she was busy with teas; and again in the shooting season she would have orders to provide cold lunches for the shooting parties that met in the woods that top the crests of the slopes round about. 'The gen'lemen,' my aunt would call them. 'I've a luncheon for the gen'lemen.' And she would make my mouth water by the hour as she sat in the back room telling me what she provided for the guns: cold veal pies, cold chicken pies, bread and cheese, home-cured ham, cheesecakes, barrels of beer, flasks of coffee, bottles of brandy. God knows how many shooting lunches I've eaten in imagination as I sat there in the back room with her.

Not that I have never eaten meals there in reality. Tea would be laid on summer afternoons on the long table in the back room, the windows open on to the garden, and the smell of thyme would come in and mingle itself with the smell of tea and seed cake and butter and that eternal soft beery smell that nothing could drive away.

There was always a perpetual coolness about the rooms at the back of the house. They faced north, over the yard that was more like a farm yard than a pub yard, with its long since disused stables and the pigeon house without pigeons and the gate leading straight into the sloping fields. They were rather dark and shadowy rooms, the whitewash faintly smoke-stained, the glass-ringed tables of scrubbed deal not reflecting even what little light there was.

It was the front room, the private room, that was the glory and pride of my aunt's house. As I see her in black, so I see this room in perpetual sunlight. It was a museum. I can think of no other way of describing it. Into it my aunt had put, year after year, all her cherished belongings. The faded gold-and-blue wallpaper was hung with the faded portraits of my family in all its branches, from stupefied-looking gents in dicky bits down to my mother in a neck ruffle as the belle of her day. There were various portraits of my deceased uncle in various attitudes of vague alarm or pride or dreaminess or statuesque melancholy. There were countless wedding groups and cricket teams, the women wearing the oddest pancake hats, the cricketers all looking slightly boss-eyed, unreal, and extremely proud of their pimple cricket caps and their waxed moustaches.

The furniture of the room was of some wood that was neither maplewood nor walnut, but somewhere between the two: a delicate deep golden wood, highly polished and grained and beautiful. The chairs were upholstered in black American leather, slippery as a straw stack. One sat on them and gradually, slowly and serenely, one slipped out of them. The table, covered with little wool mats, was of the same wood, a perfect golden oval, on which a beer stain would have been a sacrilege. On the mantelpiece were more photographs, generally head-and-shoulder portraits of the dead or miniatures of small Victorian

infants who looked as if they wished they had never been born. And on the mantelpiece, and also on all the tables and niches and ottomans and tea caddies stood countless little vases and trinkets of porcelain or milky glass, and shells and shell boxes from distant seasides. And finally, in the long bow window, the geraniums. They were very old plants; and they had grown up into miniature trees covered with flowers of hunting-pink or scarlet or wine, and here and

there with white flowers blotched and streaked with purple and rose. They were so tall and thick that they might have kept out the sunlight. For some reason they never did. It filtered through their leaves and blossoms in long shafts, not only lighting up the room but warming it, so that it had the strange fusty smell of things preserved for countless years.

I don't suppose the port at *The Chequers* was ever more than four-and-six a bottle; or the sherry. But if anyone wanted port or sherry to drink I fancy they were shown into this room like honoured guests. Other rooms could have their public ribaldry and darts and arguments and eating matches. But not this room. It was select and private. There was a kind of musty holiness there among the trinkets and the geraniums.

I mention eating matches. Once, in the early days, my aunt had tolerated an eating match. Great crowds came to see two men sit down to a couple of mountainous steaks in the smoke room. My aunt was an excellent cook and the two men ate and continued to eat until she, fearing to have a corpse if not two on her hands, hastily and prematurely declared the winner.

It was, I imagine, nothing unusual. All sorts and classes of men called at my aunt's pub, regularly or casually; the gen'lemen themselves, labourers, butchers and bakers, blacksmiths, peddling drapers, poachers, commercial travellers, shoemakers, and always strangers, who came once and never came again.

And if I remember any one thing about the place more than another it is the arrival of three strangers who asked to be shown into the private room on a summer Saturday evening. I see them now, with their black bowler hats pushed back on their sweat-ringed heads, their coats open, their watch chains dangling, and I can hear my aunt saying:

'And what could I get you, gen'lemen?'

'Whisky,' one said. 'And a jug of water.'

'Ditto,' the second said.

'Ditto,' said the third.

And when my aunt had taken in the whisky and the water and the glasses I chanced to go along the passage and see them sitting there at the private room table, their hats still on, their chairs tipped forward, their voices lowered, all watering their whisky with a kind of parsimonious secrecy and making strange patterns with their fingers on the tabletop between the intervals of raising the jug and drinking.

Who were they? What were they doing? They seemed to me then, and still do now, something like a cross between nonconformists

out for a drink on the quiet or bookmakers who had welshed and
had come to celebrate or drown their horsey sorrows. Whoever they
were they sat there hour after hour, still talking, still making their
patterns on the golden table top, still watering their whisky, only
getting up and pushing their chairs back and their hats forward
when the sun had gone from the geraniums and the summer twilight
had begun to fall.

And when I remember the pub they are an inseparable part of it,
just as that shining black is inseparable from my aunt, the sun from
the geraniums, and my aunt and the pub itself from the small wood
with its ghostly companies of orchis on the hill behind.

WOODS AND THE SEA

BY JULY THE SILENCE IS BEGINNING, and the flowerlessness. Nightingale and cuckoo have finished their season, and the month comes in full of the slumbrous broken moaning of wood pigeons in the great canopies of sun-metallic leaves. I say broken, because it is broken, because it often ceases abruptly on a phrase and then after an interval, sometimes a long interval, begins where it left off – coo coo-coo coo-coo, coo-coo, coo-coo, coo – as though the bird were cooing itself into a constant daysleep in the drowsy branches. Of all notes it is the note of high summer. It has in it the monotonous soothing drowsiness of a high noon. There is something in it that drugs the blood and that in turn deepens and stupefies the silence of the day. With it, the year seems to drop off into a snooze. There comes a feeling of oh! let it go, don't worry, sit still, have five minutes in the shade, let it go, a feeling that nothing matters. The climax has been reached, the year stands still.

In the woods that feeling is more acute, perhaps, than anywhere else. There is a kind of enervating airlessness, almost a stifling and dragging, wherever there are great masses of trees in July. It is as though – perhaps actually because – the air has been sucked up by a million leaves. W. H. Hudson himself noticed this and had some comments on it in relation to the New Forest, where he felt that the great expanse of trees seemed to suck up all life and leave the mind and body and spirit as flabby as a sponge. He pointed out how pale the Hampshire people of that district looked, as though they were literally robbed of air. The New Forest has affected me in that way as early as May, long before the leaves are at their thickest, leaving me with a feeling of drowsy gloom, turning at last into antipathy, into a feeling that I hated those vast tracts of trees and must escape from them.

And here, it seems to me, is much of the secret of the charm of woods in England. A wood should never be vast. The best woods are small, a few acres in extent, not much more than copses. The word forest creates in the mind a feeling of grandeur, of something primeval. In actuality you can't get hold of it. Its vastness is at once forbidding and elusive. It goes on and on like the vast bulk of an unread book. It is a *tour de force*, but you can't be bothered to go right through it. And forests, like heavy redundant books, so often go on and on in an endless repetition of the same thing, of trees all looking alike, never breaking, only going on and on in their own darkness. In Germany the forest, as you see it going by in the train, stretches away like a kingdom of potential telegraph poles; and the straight pines, so beautiful at first, get gradually monotonous and then more monotonous and at last unbearable. You long for a break, a change, for some treeless opening on which the mind can rest. The whole effect is altogether too vast and illimitable. You stand awed by the forest, but without affection for it. There is some kind of baffling insoluble mystery about it, a primeval darkness, a secret heart that one can never get at. Many Russian writers have written of that curious, powerful sense of profound mysteriousness which forests create. They have even made it beautiful, with the result that Russian literature is almost as full of beautiful forests as it is of beautiful girls. But these 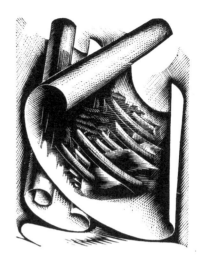 forests only exist on paper, and there are worlds of difference, for me at any rate, between the idealised forests of prose and the forests of actuality. I can love one but not the other.

Whereas, as I see it, prose can never overrate the wood: the small intimate English wood with its variation of trees, its many flowers and bird voices, its feeling of being only a part but never the whole of a countryside. It never dominates, never assumes the dark dictatorship of forests. You can walk in it and through it and round it without a sense of oppression, a sense of its being too great for you. At the same time its life is quick and, at its best, stimulating and entrancing. It is never dead, not even dormant. It is only in July that it is caught up in that lull of drugged sleepiness, of birdless noons, in the brief vacuum of high summer.

Even then there will be life going on about it, because it happens that in England cornfields and hayfields are always appearing in the heart of woods, and woods in the middle of arable and pasture country. And it is a fine thing, in July, to wander down a wood path and come suddenly upon fields full of great greenish-white seas of hay or of green corn like placid lakes that wash right up to the very foot of the woodland. Out of the wood life moves at its height. The sun stabs down with naked spears of heat, burning out the scent of hay or later, in August, the hot sweet smell of corn and stubble and sun-cracked earth, of horse sweat and man sweat and binder oil and tractor fumes, all the smells of animation, of man in contact with the earth, of man and earth in contact with the sun. It is a life almost as far removed from the life of the wood as night from day. In the wood, on the fiercest noons, there is a coldness and stillness and shadowiness under the trees that is like a momentary oasis of death. For a moment or two, after the sickening blaze of sunlight, the wood is a relief, but before long that utter completeness of shade begins to seem unfriendly, then forbidding, and finally hostile. It is too complete. It is like the forethrown shadow of winter. Against the quivering sweet heat of open stubbles the wood seems damp – is damp. It has in it already a breath of the faint odours of autumn, of dying. For, in spite of the everlasting lively presence of squirrels in the oaks and pines, there is already a feeling of death in it: the flabby extinction of a million bluebell spikes, fat-seeded, the yellowing of primrose leaves, the black spilling down of foxglove seed. Only the bracken is in its lush maturity, and, in cleared spaces, the bay willowherb, half seed, half flower, the bracken strawberry-scented, the willowherb crushed strawberry-coloured except for its fluffed white heads of cotton seed.

And it is a relief to get out into the open again, to see the sky, to be stabbed by heat, to see green corn or yellow corn or hay or the dark metallic-leaved acres of roots, shining almost like tropical plants in the sun. The wood is best now, in early August, from outside, as a dark tree-background to the low curtain of almost copper wheat or of the pale green, not yet straw hat coloured barley. And soon afterwards there comes a great time, the best of all in the English

later summer, when corn is half cut everywhere, some cut and lying in sheaf, some standing in ear and some in shock, so that the land all about is like the camping ground of a vast army just pitching its tents. It is the first fusing of summer and autumn: of stalk and stubble, green sloe and blue, the seed and fingers of honeysuckle, red blackberry and black, and, in the woods, of the green and yellow of full leaf and dying.

It is not much, but it is there, the first sign: a vein of yellow, a mere peppering of bronze, nothing. It is no more noticeable than the solitary grey hairs of a man in full maturity. The woods still look solid and powerful and lush. They stand as though eternal, carved imperishably out of some vast block of everlasting greenheart. They seem, against the yellow and copper and white of harvest fields, as evergreen as holly or bay. They take the quick change interludes of autumn without ever seeing the change themselves. The earth tires visibly under the sun, the grassland is arid; or the wheat lies swamped and smashed under the rollers of storm. But nothing affects the woods. They stand about the landscape with the gloomy solidity of monuments.

As always, they have their beauty. But in August it is sombre. It has lost the quickness and light of youth. It is then that woods by water come into their own, woods by quick-moving brooks, woods by placid-moving and water-lilied rivers, and, finest of all, woods by the sea.

They are not common. The coast, in England, is anybody's playground, and we are a nation, not of shopkeepers, but of jerry builders, masters of the art of destroying what we most profess to love. And ironically enough, the English coast is well suited to this vandalism. Its flats and headlands and lawn-covered cliffs are paradises for those who make profits out of the common human desire for escape – that out-of-nowhere-into-nothing kind of escape which drives people from jerry-built towns inland to jerry-built towns by the sea. Had the English coast been wooded and had it, more important, been held in trust for everlasting for the nation and its people I might now be writing a chapter on its unique glory. But woods by the English sea are rarities. I rejoice whenever I see them, which is not often. The spaces for woods along the English coastline, never vast, are being crushed out of existence, and with them, if it comes to that, the spaces for field and hedge and farm and tree and stream. Here, as inland, the English are playing with masterly stupidity the game of picking their own pockets – a new expression, no doubt, of their innate passion, practised now for centuries, for picking other people's.

What woods there still are, therefore, by the English sea, will not be sanctuaries of untrampled quietness in August. But that combination of trees and sea is still irresistible: the trees running down thickly by gorge and stream valley to the very edge of sand and rock, the trees themselves bent into the savage toughened shapes of lop-sided umbrellas, as though flattened back by some colossal flat-iron of storm and wind. And far below, beyond the trees, the sea shining with that flashing sun-hard glitter of August, making a mind-drowsy distance of water and light, the silence under the stunted trees broken by the everlasting break of waves and the mewing of gulls and the sudden paper-rustling sound of small sea winds, eddying and dying in trees and in sea pinked clefts of cliff somewhere out of sight.

POACHERS AND MUSHROOMS

No SOONER IS CORN CUT AND STUBBLE BARE than the young
pheasants are released in tame flocks along the woodsides.
Mothered all summer long by stupid hens, they are rather like large
stupid brown chickens themselves. They grow with great rapidity,
chickens one week, timorous and fussy and uncertain even on the
wide stubbles, strutting like young bloods the next, with the first
sign of pheasant-arrogance that reaches its height at the end of
September, when cocks stroll across the roads with the damnable
proud indifference of peacocks, savagely scarlet and electric blue
and wild-looking and yet, ironically, almost as tame as ducks on an
orchard pond. The pheasant occupies an odd position in English bird
life. It is the royal pretender, the pampered scarlet-crowned would-
be king of every field and wood. Fussed and pampered and protected
from all manner of evil by armed guards, he leads the sheltered life
of a royal heir, and all for one purpose. By some ironical chance
he bears the sign of that purpose on his head, in the fierce scarlet

side-splashes that might be his inheritance of spilt blood. Though he struts like a royal pretender he is, from egg onwards, one thing, and one thing only. He is the lamb to the slaughter.

And in September, as in spring, he makes the woods places of miserable uneasiness. You must not go near, you must not look at him. However respectable and sweet and harmless you may be, you are a potential killer. You may even be, which is worse, a potential poacher.

Because, by the unalterable law of have and have-not, the poacher comes into his heyday when the pheasant comes into his. The one, in a sense, has produced the other. I will not say that, by abolishing the pheasant, you would also abolish the poacher. The poacher is something more than this; he is a survival, bang in the middle of civilisation of primitive man, of the hunter in the wild. With the fisherman, he is the last of a race hunting by its own skill, and for its own joy and profit, the wild creatures of earth. He is even one above the fisherman, that is the freshwater fisherman, who now generally puts fish into the water before he can hope to pull any out again. The poacher has one other distinction: he is the only survivor, now that the smuggler has gone, of the romantic thief, of the hunter who is himself hunted.

It is, altogether, an exciting craft. What could be more exciting, at any rate in this now placid, smooth-shaven, no longer wild countryside of ours? The poacher works by night, in the difficulty of darkness, by primitive methods, on other people's land. He runs considerable risk, even the supreme risk. He needs great courage, delicate and specialised skill, and some kind of inborn love and understanding and appetite, some kind of shifty hunger for wildlife and air. His craft is only thieving by chance. He is driven primarily by some irrepressible instinct for excitement and danger, by some love of wild pursuit for which he is not consciously responsible.

I have never believed that sheer want or an instinct of rebellion against society ever drove a man to poaching. I was brought up in a town notorious for its poachers: an industrial town of nearly fifteen thousand people, with all the respectable paraphernalia of churches and societies and brass bands and bands of brothers. Also, a prosperous town, a town in which the girls are as smart as models and in which the streets of anything like real squalor at all can be counted on the fingers of one hand. A town also with an extreme civic consciousness and respectability.

And also, twenty-five or thirty or forty years ago, swarming with poachers, master craftsman shoemakers, most of them, who could earn, because they were master craftsmen working in their own time and at their own leisure, what money they pleased within the limits of their trade. All shoemakers by day and poachers by night. What drove them? Clearly not money. It came into it, but it was not paramount. Also not hatred of the squire, since personal contact between squire and poacher was almost non-existent. The two, often, never saw each other. They lived at a distance, in different worlds. If there was any hatred at all it was between poacher and keeper, which was the result of and not the cause of poaching. Nor was the pheasant itself the cause. Rabbits did just as well; anything did just as well – hares, partridges, pigeons, even fox cubs, even young badgers to bring home and keep for a day or two in the old backyard hen roost. Anything did; anything to hunt or capture or kill with a reasonable chance of excitement. It was the expression of a primitive instinct, so strong that it took men beyond the confines of their legitimate occupation into a chancy occupation that could and did entail prison and wounding and even, remotely, death.

Have you ever eaten a poached pheasant? It tastes very good. It seems in some way more piquant than the plucked and skewered bird delivered by the poulterer. This is pure fancy, of course, but

there is some sweet relish in eating a poached bird, just as there is in eating a scrumped apple. My aunt, at the small white pub already described, often exchanged an honest quart for a dishonest bird and pursed her severe lips and looked at the sky and said nothing. Hares, too, and rabbits, still blood-warm as they slid over the bar. And all the time looking as though she never put a toenail over the chalk line of right and respectability.

So, in September, the poacher starts. Darkness begins to come down earlier and it is the protection of darkness above all that he wants, and in fact the only protection he can hope to get. The woods also are regaining their life. The summer vacuum of bird silence and shadowiness has been broken. The life is flowing again – back now, really ebbing, like the sap itself. In the woods, especially, life and sap are synonymous. It is that uprising of sap in April and May, and even March, that gives woods their beautiful and stimulating sense of life. It is the flowing back, the slow return to death and the bottom of the pit, that gives them in autumn that peculiar air of soft melancholy, the infusion of sad odours and the sweet death of uncountable leaves.

In late September the full fruition of things has come: wood nuts hanging pale green among the already formed and even paler green next-year's catkins, black ripening of elderberries and blackberries, the first bloodiness of honeysuckle berry and bryony and even hip and haw, the greening of sweet chestnuts, the cupping of acorns. The trees are thinning, not much, imperceptibly, and the light is coming in. The stitches in the leaf canopy are breaking and rotting. There is a casual soundless spinning down of first leaves.

Dimly, not yet at their best, the parasols of fungus are opening. They will be at their finest, roughly, with the sweet chestnuts, on darker and softer days of humid rain. Meanwhile, it is the great season, in the meadows beyond the wood, for mushrooms. They will even grow in the wood, but not often, and they are not good there.

I am speaking now of the common mushroom, almost the only fungus we in England eat.

If the weather is right, that is if there are sultry nights and rains and warm moons, that mushroom, *Agaricus campestris*, is generally in season somewhere between August and November, though with the same weather it will spring up unexpectedly, sometimes, at hay-time, almost lost in the long mowing grass. In England these are its only seasons. I am aware that quantities of cultivated fungi, much resembling miniature umbrellas cut out of old bat's wings, are sold in the shops all the year round, Christmas or Easter, moon or no moon, at distressing prices. But I am speaking of mushrooms – the wild, tender, beautiful pink-gilled meadow mushrooms that are like little white silk parasols come out of children's tales.

There is really no other mushroom except this, the wild one. A mushroom grown in a hothouse or in the darkness of a disused

coal mine is a tasteless and almost artificial thing in comparison. A mushroom, a real mushroom, is dew-tasty, faintly fragrant of autumn earth, as fresh as morning rain. A mushroom in a shop is in fact like a bird in a cage. A pound of mushrooms, please – the words, for a countryman, are almost blasphemous. As well ask for a bouquet of buttercups at a florist's, a brace of jackdaws at a poulterer's, as for a pound of mushrooms at a greengrocer's on an autumn morning.

Ask for them, of course, if you must and if you will, but more than half your delight is gone at once if you do: not the delight of eating them or the delight of cooking them, but the incomparable delight of gathering them. And without doubt it is an incomparable delight. Against it the gathering of blackberries is a barbaric and doubtful pleasure of stains and thorns, the picking of sloes and crab apples a sour-belly business, without a thrill of unexpectedness or expectation. Bend down the briar, shake the tree – like the tail of the snail, that's all there is in it. Not so with mushrooms. A likely mushroom field is one with patches of long tussocky grass interspersed with little green horse-dunged lawns, or an old hayfield where the grass has begun to grow thick and sweet with autumn rain. But there is no certainty about it. The gathering of mushrooms is all chance and hope.

And the chances are that when the field is found someone will have been there before you. But just as likely not. It is all uncertainty. There is a tradition that to gather mushrooms you must be up and about, like a rook, at five o'clock in the morning. I have never believed it and have never done it, though I have gathered more mushrooms than perhaps I deserve for scorning the rule. Let the shepherd and the poacher have them early in the morning. For my part I like the evening, with the fading and not the rising light, the falling dew, the flocks of starlings flying over in the stillness, the rabbits feeding quietly on the edge of the wood, the soft, elusive, indefinable smell of the evening itself, and above all the pure whiteness of the mushrooms shining out of the darkening grass in the twilight.

Here, then, is the perfect time. You climb the fence, you begin to wander in the damp field, there is something that shines very white in the grass ahead. You advance, you unclasp the knife, you pause and stoop. A tuft of sheep's wool. It is the first of a thousand trickeries that light and distance will play on you. The field will become full of little whitenesses that will deceive you again and again: white thistle seeds, white flint and stones, a scrap of paper, a late moon daisy, a

puffball, a sun-blanched leaf, groups of white convolvulus, the white heads of yarrow flowers. You will grow tired and maddened and finally cunning and wary, understanding why it is easier to gather blackberries. In time, also, you will begin to distinguish between one white and another, between a thistle seed and a flower, between a flower and a mushroom. The faintest wind will shake the thistle seed and the flower, but the mushroom is immovable. And there is nothing to match the purity of its whiteness, the living silky candescence that can be visible across the whole width of a darkening field.

There is no mistaking a mushroom: first there is no other fungus with a skin just so white and silken, secondly there is nothing else in the world, not even a flamingo or a rose, that has the same pinkness as the undergills of a new-grown mushroom. It is an absolute perfection of colour blending: a little crimson, some white, a mistiness of purple. And as though that were not enough, the gills, broken delicately as they run inwards towards the fat white stalk, give to it all the softest shimmering effect like that of shot silk.

After the gathering, then the eating. To come home in the autumn twilight, to peel the mushrooms, to cook, to eat – they are the delights that come next to the gathering. And just as there is only one true mushroom there is, to my mind, only one true way in which to eat it. The cookery books will give you a thousand finicky devices, mushrooms in this, mushrooms in that, but there is only one way – to fry them, simply with bacon, until they swim in their black fragrant juice. It is the way of the shepherd and the poacher, the way of all true mushroomers since ever there were horses and fields and autumn moons.

THE HEART OF AUTUMN

SUMMER AND AUTUMN fuse into each other imperceptibly, the point of fusion lost in some period of September humidity, in a mild wonder of too-soft days. Autumn comes slowly, and having come slowly, goes on slowly, for a long time, even as far on as December. In a country of many trees, such as this is, where one kind of tree turns its colours while another holds them fast and where some trees are stripped while others are summered with leaf, it is never easy to make the mark between season and season. Autumn slips a finger into August, but spring has a revenge in December. Winter blows on September, but October still remains, with May and June, the loveliest month of the English year, a kind of second spring, uncertain but exhilarating, sunny and snowy, hot and frosty, bright and dark by turns, a sort of autumnal April.

With it, the woods are at their best again. On some day in late October, after a night of frost, the sweet chestnuts come showering down like prickled apples, splitting against the boughs as they fall, opening to cream-coloured cups in which the chestnuts lie tight-sandwiched, like fat mahogany peardrops. But generally, so early, there is no breaking of the cup and the nut case lies almost as inviolable on the ground as on the tree, a fierce ball of pricks needing courage and strength to break. The gathering of these nuts is a great business in the south. The woods become places of pilgrimage, not so much for the country folk, who have an astonishing disregard for the fruits of the earth lying at their back doors, as for the townsfolk. Out they come, by bus and car and bike, principally men, very earnest, and principally on Sunday mornings. It is a piece of yearly ritual. They raid the woods like human squirrels, spending hours kneeling or stooping or even sitting under the canopy of leaves already much thinned by rain and frost, foraging among the blanket of fallen leaf and husk, filling cans and sacks with the silk-soft nuts, staggering out at last under the weight of their pot-bellied sacks, still looking very earnest but, somehow, satisfied.

And since it is a kind of common ritual, off we go too: infants and pram and basket and bags and the lot. We also like the nuts, though not ravenously. Still, it does not matter. Once in the wood, we are like the rest. We kneel and sit and stoop under the great trees and split open the fat emerald shells and gather the mahogany harvest. There is a great smell of autumn everywhere: great in the literal sense, an all-pervading, powerful odour, universal and bountiful, that changeless autumn formula of warmth and wet, of drip and decay. In the heart of the wood it is thick and drowsy, almost a fermentation. It drowses and drunkens everything.

The two infants are small and feminine. They wear pantaloons of blue or pink silk, about as large as decent paper bags, that are just not adequate enough to cover their pink bottoms. They stagger and stumble on small legs and flop and half-drown in the thick sea of fallen leaves and husks. They are both fair, with hair four or five shades lighter than primroses. But on the one it is straight as grass and on the other it curls like a thousand silky sweet pea

tendrils. I foresee for them a future of distinguished devilry. With the faces of angels, they have the world weighed up. They are beyond all hoodwinking or cheating or delusion. It's all a game, and their parents, like the Spanish chestnuts, are just part of it.

And down there, in the wood one day, tired of gathering chestnuts, they roamed and gathered something else: many umbrellas of fungus. It was my first revelation of the range and brilliance of English fungi. That afternoon we gathered them of all sizes from the size of a pearl button to a football, in all colours from white to black, from cream to purple, from yellow to scarlet. They grew everywhere, under leaves and on dead wood and living, lifting up pads of decayed leaf and earth, forcing their way past fallen trunks and up through tangles of briar and living leaf. They filled the wood with their sombre rotten-sweet odour of decay. We gathered boleti that were like sponge cakes: greenish olive-yellow underneath, or faint rose, or creamy white. The infants returned triumphant with scarcely visible infantile parasols of old-maidish dingy mauve or brown. We found many little clavaria of mauve and pink and white, like sea coral, small branching stems of almost untouchable delicacy. And everywhere silk-gilled parasols of sepia and cream and pigeon-grey and stone-colour; and suddenly some rarer, quite dazzling specimens in orange or scarlet or crimson or purple, big and gaudy; and rarer still some yellow-bellied thing, something of slimy lizardish green or a strange, too-pure sinister white.

And all under the birches, large and small, tight and flaunting, that too-handsome *Amanita muscaria*, like a Russian cake in looks and somehow like a Russian villainess by name, poisonously scarlet, and decorated, like some precious cake, with its rich flecks of almond. This Amanita, the fly agaric, is said to be eaten in Russia, though extremely poisonous. But then the Russians, to whom fungi are like a creed, will eat anything. In Russia, too, Amanita is said to be used, like hashish in the East, as a means of drugged intoxication. Gathered and dried, it has some powerful narcotic effect. Moreover, one fungus goes a long way, since the power of it will continue, with a tiny extra daily fillip, for a week. There is generally much needless panic, among country folk especially, regarding fungus. But Amanita justifies it. Under the quiet birches, on the soft rain-mild October days, she is somehow too brilliant. She looks sinister, and that lovely dome-shaped cake, poppy-scarlet, is deadly.

With fungus and nuts and the spinning seeds of sycamore, the autumn reaches its heart. We talk of the height of summer, the dead of winter, the fullness of spring. But autumn reaches a heart, a core of fruitfulness and decline, that has in it the sweet dregs of the year. Under the quiet skies the woods stand now with a kind of contradictory magnificence: gaudy and smouldering, flaring and almost arrogant, the stain of yellow and bronze spreading and deepening among the green, the copper flames of beeches firing whole sections of the woods with stationary heatless fires that look perpetual. Even the green now is burning. It has the yellow of flame in it. It bears some faint relation to the green flames of fires on nights of frost. And when frost comes now, it is paradoxically not to extinguish or lessen these vast flames of leaf, but to sting them into a finer richness and fierceness. The wood in the lane, more birch and oak than anything, smoulders only in a continual cloud of yellow. It is the woods on the hills, with their great structures of beech and larch, that make the vast day-fires of copper and orange and even, sometimes, crimson, all flame except for the plaything tufts of wild clematis seed tangled on the outer edges of the wood, little sheep wool tufts of still smoke that even the rage of winter never quite blows away.

And now there is also a kind of second spring of flowers. In the woods it is honeysuckle mostly, cool and now almost white-fingered and unseen as it hangs among young chestnut and hazel. On the woodsides it is the final flush of willowherb, the last creaming of meadowsweet in the ditches, the last petticoat-pink rags of campion. By the waterside willowherb also goes on, and meadowsweet, and a few solitary magenta brushes of loosestrife. There is no flush of bloom. Wherever it is, it is accidental, modest, an aftermath. It is symbolic in every way of autumn, which is not so much a season of itself as a remembrance and a foretaste of seasons. The year distils itself into October. Rain and sun and frost and wind and death act like balm, so that there is a miraculous clarifying and softening of everything, until the limpid days are like wine.

And as the month ends there is not only a change in the feeling of
the days but in the habit of them. Pheasants, a little less tame now,
not quite tame enough to catch in the hand, are ripe for shooting,
and the fox lies bored to death, summer-sick, not yet roused to the
heat of mating passion, in hidden holes under the oak roots in wood
and spinney. And since something must be done to fill the empty
days of fox and bird, we begin to see, almost any afternoon now,
the troops of riders that call themselves the hunt and the platoons of
baggy trousers that call themselves the shoot. The fact that many of
them cannot ride and that many of them, even sober, could not hit
a haystack does not matter. They are the missionaries of excitement.
Without them the land, and the woods in particular, would slip into
a kind of living death of boredom.

The English hunt is a great institution. I say it seriously. Where
else is there such noble compatibility between man and beast as
here between horse and rider, such tempered courage, such beauty
of clean-limbed goddesses and strength of men? If I do not always
see these virtues displayed in the various hunts that go lolloping and
straggling and careering over the young wheat in winter, it is, no
doubt, not because I see some kind of exceptional hunt lacking such
qualities, but only because I, plebeian by birth and upbringing, have
a habit of looking at things in a cockeyed way. That accounts for the
fact, no doubt, that the women of the hunts I see always seem less
like goddesses than painted whores on horseback, and that there is
less strength of men than of potbellied beeriness and belching and
monocled haw-hawing of hardened boozer and bully. For I never
saw such ill-sitting, rampaging, ill-assorted collections of amateur
whores and dowagers and snobs and mongrels and butcher-faces as
collect about English villages and fields from October to April for
the purpose of enjoying the Great Sport. There are those who have

cruelty as their prime reason against the hunt – cruelty to the fox. To me there is only one cruelty – cruelty to the horse. It seems to me a piece of barbaric cruelty to expect of that noble animal that it shall carry the ignoble burdens that grace it, top-hatted or pink-coated, at the hunt meets up and down these islands. I have nothing against the sport. It is a great sport, a magnificent sport. It is extremely exciting; it brings about a refining and ennobling of the instincts. The only thing that would make it more exciting and perhaps more refining and ennobling is the substitution of a cow, say, for the fox, the cow to be maddened in milk and to have the privilege, if necessary, of goring the horses. The whole thing could then be made more domestic; we could all join, without compunction, in a cow hunt. It would be more democratic. And if the cow were killed what matter? We could have extra beef on Sundays. A fox cannot be eaten. Why therefore hunt it? The hunting of cows would, on the other hand, show a sound economic purpose.

But these are reforms which I can never hope to see accomplished in my lifetime. The hunt as we know it meanwhile goes on, the last relic of English feudal snobbery: pink coat and side-saddle and veil and beef face, and, of course, the grooms. The English groom has, unlike many of the ladies for whom he brings fresh mounts, something in common with the Venus de Milo. He is a piece of immortal and broken statuary. The face of an English groom is unequalled and unrivalled by any other face in the world. Poker faces, inscrutable Chinese, convicts, gangsters, lawyers, dictators, jockeys – they have nothing on the groom. It is a face of remarkable impassivity. It seems emotionless. And yet, somehow, you have the feeling that it conceals, by habit, by force, by fear, by some means somehow, the most complex emotions. What is it that moulds a face? Grooms are not born with that pallid hardness of unemotional servility. What shapes and changes them? The horse? The lowest

kind of servitude, the servitude of man to animal, the constant
reminder that horses are almost gods and grooms less than dogs? Is
it a kind of contrabalancing, a levelling up? Is it because there is just
so much nobility and none to spare between horse and man and that
the horse takes it all? There are times when it seems to me like some
gross sort of love affair, with the horse like a woman sucking out the
last drop of the man's decency. Whatever it is it creates that baffling
countenance: the bloodless, soulless, inscrutable, pathetic groom-face
of tradition. It creates also one of the oddest paradoxes that any visitor
to England is ever likely to see: the sight of groom with horse, the bit
of broken human statuary on the back of the wine-veined, almost
wine-fed animal, of human servility against animal mastery.

So the hunt cries and yelps and hollers about these quiet fields all
winter. There is some stag hunting and otter hunting too. In the early
year the stags in the park beyond the road, a quarter of a mile away,
roar with passionate rutting voices. The herd is about fifty strong and

occasionally, down in the wood, there will be a new sound of feet in the quietness, a dainty stepping among dead leaves, too heavy for pheasant or fox: a stray escaped doe, perhaps two, dapple-shadowy under the trees, by the river. They are never easy to see. They are the exact silvery fawn colour of the dead sweet chestnut leaves, with darker splashes, and standing among the trees, in the freckly sunlight, they tone away into invisibility. Until suddenly they are roused. And then they start up and are off, electrically, with amazing lightness and speed, almost ethereally, vanishing miraculously or halting far down in the wood, at a safe distance, silly-timid, wonderfully dainty, the prettiest creatures the wood ever knows.

WINTER GALE AND WINTER SPRING

W<small>E ARE NEAR THE SEA</small>, and there is sea on three sides of us, to south and south-east and to somewhere between east and north. The hills, with their great barricades of trees, shut us off from north and north-east, but between us and the Channel there is nothing but the bare plain of weald and marsh. And when in November the wind turns to south-west and is whipped into the sudden fury of autumnal storm, nothing can stop it. It roars up the Channel and over marsh and weald, and strikes us with whining frenzy out of a racing tempestuous sky. The clouds hurl over us very low down and thick and furious and the rain is lashed out of them in torrential streams, rarely cold and more rarely bitter, but a great howling blustering wateriness, warm and sea-heavy, that has in it a kind of smashing exultation. That November storm is almost unfailing in its yearly recurrence; it comes with the regularity of March winds and the Indian summer of October. It is the year's greatest and most furious piece of transformation. Its blast changes the whole character of the land from mellowness to barrenness; it strips off the last flesh of autumn leaves, smashes out the last breath of summer.

The sound of it is exactly like the sea: the constant implacable beating of wave against shore that has in it something glorious and relentless. The beating of wind and rain against the woods makes a grand sea sound somehow appropriate to the almost catastrophic change it brings: the fierce baring of boughs, the mighty herding up of leaves, the whole cyclonic cleansing away of the remnants of death. In a single day or night the woods are changed beyond recognition. There is a sudden great letting in of light. Frost has rotted the stitches of the canopy of leaves, but not irrevocably. They still cling there, the oaks especially, with a pretence of permanence. The storm tears them out completely, lashes them into nothingness, annihilates the whole fabric of them. They are driven away like crowds of multitudinous small birds, in wild whirlwinds and swooping flocks in air and in rolling and spinning and somersaulting crowds along the earth. And with them are driven away the sweetish damp death-odours of autumn itself. The air is whipped into a rain-freshness, a new clear coldness, the first touch of winter that is as exhilarating as spring.

This storm lasts, sometimes, for as long as half a week. After it the leaves are piled up in brown and yellow mountains everywhere, thigh-deep. The sweet chestnut leaves are like great ragged scraps of fawn paper; the beech are like copper shavings, brittle and shiny and upcurled, as though ripped off with a colossal plane. Sycamore and poplar are like flat and slippery yellow fish. Birch are like dead butterflies, oak like scorched paper. The wood is full of them. If thousands were driven away into nothingness, millions remain. There is no longer any wonder why the wood, at midsummer, was almost sunless. The thickness of leaves raises the wood floor, now, anything up to a foot. No wonder its living green blotted out the sky.

And now, after the storm, the sight of the first clearing of the sky from beneath the trees is very fine. Rain-washed, cleared of cloud, it is pale blue, infinitely clear, with a kind of pure morning clarity. The first wintry beauty of trees is enhanced by it. Trees stand out, at last, with their own characters, oak knotty, birch thready, ash spindly and looping. There is suddenly a remarkable grace about them, a laciness, a pattern. Yet together, from afar off, they have the permanence of iron. They are iron-coloured. Frost and rain alone changes them, frost to silver, rain to bronze and steel. They give the land a sense of rich solidity even in the deadness of winter; they are living veins of tree-ore running about the cropless fields and the vacant pastures. More than anything they save the land from barrenness.

Suddenly, in early December, the land seems strangely quiet and still. There is a sultriness as soft as milk over everything. There are brief spells of damp, windless weather, after rain, when whole days seem like soundless preludes to spring. The grass in pastures is thick and rich with an almost spring greenness and the trees stand out with new delicacy and colour against the half dark sky: fresh skeletoned shapes of black and red and grey and softest brown, the willows and osiers varnished a deep walnut, the trunks of sycamore and chestnut stained over with a silvery green fungus which clings to them like bright damp pollen, the smooth bark of the dogwood as warm as claret against the harsh twigs of blackthorn. The branches of the trees are as still as death. The air is soft and mild and the distance half-obscured with lingering mist, so that the colours of the bare woods are dissolved into one colour, the tender blue of still smoke or shadows on snow.

This wet stillness and the silent immobility of things create a brief sense of spring. The land seems in suspense. Nothing is happening:

but it is as though something is about to happen. The suspense is full of mystery and expectation. Great white raindrops hang heavy and motionless on all the winter-blackened twigs of sloe and birch and bramble and haw, like new snowdrop buds of glass. There is no sound or wind or sunshine: no light except in the suspended rain on the still boughs in the wet still air. The light in the air itself is very dull, the clouds woven windlessly into a single fabric of cloud from one misty horizon to another; but the light in the raindrops, imprisoned, as though distilled, is wonderful. It seems to belong to another time: to spring itself. Yet there is no sunshine in it: only a clear transparent winter light, as still as death, glistening and gleaming like morning ice.

This extraordinary stillness and suspense creates a strange feeling of melancholy. Much has been written of the joy of spring, but very little of its melancholy. Yet the earliest sense of spring, coming with the first light cold evenings of February, or with the weak sunlight of flowerless January afternoons or with these periods of mild suspense in December, is filled with an indefinable sadness. It is one of the oddest and sometimes one of the most charming characteristics of English weather that at times one season borrows complete days from another, spring from summer, winter from spring. And it may be that these milky days of winter, which seem borrowed from April, are automatically filled with the sadness of things out of their time.

Or it may have nothing to do with these things at all: but only with ourselves, with our own sudden nostalgia for the sunlight. Is there anything spring-like after all in the dark wet days, the leafless boughs, the flowerless grass, the bare distances and that empty sunless sky? The sheep lands, with the muddy sheep gnawing desultorily among the winter turnips, are dreary wastes of flattened mud scattered with black and green trails of sheep droppings and turnip stalks and printed with the narrow rain-filled patterns of sheep tracks. Looking

at the sheep and the squares of hurdles on the desolate turnip land, faced that is with something requiring no leap of imagination to see or feel, we lose completely the illusion of spring.

It is only imagination which can and does bring it back again. A sudden breath of soft air, the crowing of a cockerel, the cry of a blackbird: some sudden startling tiny thing quickens the mind into recreation.

Not that there are no material signs of spring. Above the quiet wintry

water of rivers and ponds and lakes, with their gatherings and sudden uprisings of wild duck, the willows and osiers have assumed a burning loveliness, their buds long and sharp as though ready to break. And in the sheltered copses of hazel and sweet chestnut the primroses are budded or half-opened, shining scraps of moonlight in the wet black leaf mould. Something seems not only about to happen, but in fact to be happening. The buds are awake before they are asleep. There is a grain of reality in the illusory spring, the faintest movement and change in the apparently motionless and changeless air of the silent winter day.

And there is, also, a small separate and actual spring in December: something apart from illusion and the chance buds of primroses and the flaming buds of willow trees. In December the evergreens reach their April. On the edges of game preserves, in the parks of the well-to-do, in the old mixed south country hedges, the richness of holly berries against the even greater richness of holly leaves is a perpetual delight. And in the parks the dark groups and corridors of cypress and box and yew take on a rich and sombre glory, melancholy and entrancing as the sense of spring itself, that they never know in summer. If there is one thing I envy above all others in the mansions and parks of the rich it is the glory of their yews and cypresses, soft green and black and yellow and blue and emerald, impassive and quiet trees, planted with thought and prodigality by someone in another and more lavish age. They stand out with singular life and loveliness against the cloudy sky and the naked deciduous trees and, above all, against the expanses of fox-coloured bracken drenched with rain. And in the still winter air they seem to be stiller than all other trees: dark static columns, funereal but lovely, inseparable and unchangeable parts of the wintry land and the suspended winter silence that seems also as if it can never change or break.

It does break, however, at last. The wind rises and changes, the still raindrops are shaken from the boughs, the bare trees are lashed with sudden fury, the south-west wind cries in the house and the trees again with the old eternal moaning melancholy, and the brief December spring is gone.

THE SNOWS OF SPRING

A ND SOMEHOW, however pleasant, that winter spring has
something ominous about it. It is too quiet, far too soft. It has
in it something of the dangerous placidity of a sleeping lion. While it
lasts fields are too green, woods stand too still. In any other country
than this, perhaps, it would mean nothing. But in England the weather
is like a fitful beast: inconsequent and unreliant and treacherous and
changing all the time, stormy and sweet, hot and bitter quicker than a
jealous woman. There is no knowing what is coming next. The days
are fickle. The seasons are turned upside down.

And so, in England, snow and flowers are common enough
together; in April the wallflowers will often be laid like corn, the
plum blossom dissolved and the tulips transformed to satin snow
cups by sudden blinding storms of white, driven against the sunshine.
And earlier, in March or even February, the crocuses are caught wide
open, like ground stars of purple and gold and white, catching the
first flakes in their orange hearts before suddenly shutting up, stiff

and tight, like flowers of coloured glass, imperishable and unearthly. Snow, next to flowers and sunshine and perhaps the rainbow, is the loveliest of all natural events, certainly the loveliest of all winter happenings, lovelier than frost or winter moonlight. And in England it comes seldom enough to be a rare joy and never lingers long enough to be wearisome. It falls and performs its brief white miracle of transformation and vanishes again before the senses have grown used to that amazing whiteness, the beauty of blue bays of sky opening above the snow-lined trees, and the strange stillness of the silent land.

I am not talking now of the snow which falls in towns, and which is not at all the most lovely winter phenomenon, but probably the most depressing and most hated: only of snow which falls in the country, opening out in a wonderful way its distances, creating a feeling of great light and tranquil spaciousness in its open fields and a strange softness and silence in its woods, the trees never moving under the weight of snow, the bird life suspended except for the dainty pattering of pheasants among bracken and bramble and over snow-sprinkled chestnut leaves and the wild cry of a mad blackbird escaping through the hazels. There is no stillness in the world like the stillness of the world under snow. The stillness of summer is made up in effect of sounds, of many little drowsy sounds like the warm monotonous moan of pigeons, the changeless tune of invisible yellowhammers, the dreamy fluttering of thick leaves, sounds which together send the air half to sleep and create that singing silence which is almost a tangible thing in the heart of warm summer afternoons.

But the silence of snow is absolute; the silence of death and suspense. It is as though the snow has a paralysing effect, deadening the wind, freezing the voices of the birds. It is a silence which is absolutely complete in itself; not an illusion like the summer silence, not made up of sounds somnolently repeated. It is pure tranquillity and soundlessness, profoundest and most wonderful when the snow has finally ceased; full of expectancy and broken by the occasional uneasy cries of rooks when snow has still to come. And the fall of snow on snow, through the silence of snow, is the perfection of beauty: a lovely paradox of silence and movement, of stillness and life, the twinkling and fluttering and dancing of the new snow against the old.

Then, as the day goes on, the effect of tranquillity and softness lessens, and a feeling of wildness, increasing rapidly as the light dies, begins to take its place. The silence is still there, but the deadness has gone. There is life in it, a wild feeling of desolation. The air is alive with frost. Little sudden ground winds spring up with the twilight, and in the half-light the land is more than ever a white wilderness, a bitter desert of frozen drifts and dark spaces from which the snow dust has been driven. On the cornland and the colourless empty land broken up in readiness for spring sowing, where the snow is thinnest, a mere dust of whitest ice clinging to the dark clots of earth and the wind-flattened corn shoots, dark prostrate steeples and balloons of snowless earth stretch out like shadows across the fields wherever trees have broken the force of the wind and have kept the snow from the land.

The lovely white morning snow-stillness and snow-light have gone. In their place there is a desolation of wind and cloud and frost and suddenly upscattered snow, an altogether new element of wildness and bleakness, wonderful and invigorating. The old premature spring lassitude and melancholy have gone, too. The snow has transformed everything. The half spring-like colours of the green land and the warm red trees have been covered or washed out, the fields turned to white pastures, the branches of trees bearing nothing but snow-leaves and snow-buds, the hedges covered with a light spreading of

snow that is like a delicate blossoming of false blackthorn.

In the day time it was the little things that gave delight: the leaves of primrose and violet and the transparent lemon cups of winter aconite embalmed in crystal, the dead seed-plumes of grass and flowers transformed to little trees of silver, the tender blue of the snow shadows, the lace patterns of birds' feet, the whole transfiguration of leaf and twig and stone and earth. In the twilight they have no significance. The little things are blotted out, the world is wilder and altogether grander. The tearing passage of dark cloud against the orange sunset is desolate and strange and powerful. The orange light that falls on the snow and the snowy branches and the torn edges of cloud is almost savage. The snow gleams softly orange and then pink as the west changes its light, and then blue and dark as though with smoke when the light dies at last.

And there is also no longer an absence of life or movement or sound. Starlings fly constantly over in low and disordered flocks, dipping and fetting and straggling with evening fear, the multitudinous dark underwings turned briefly orange or pink by the wild sunset light, the crescendo of the flight startling in the silence. And on the cornland or ploughed land a hare will come out and lope along and pause and huddle dark against the snow, and watch the light, and then limp on again, stopping and huddling and watching until lost beyond a ridge of land at last. And in the woods there is a constant settling and unsettling of wings and feet on frozen twigs and leaves, the pheasants croaking mournfully and beating the air with frantic flacking wings, the unseen and unknown little birds fluttering in half-terror at the night and the snow.

And in the west, above the savage orange pinkish light, the first stars are more brilliant than frost against the mass of travelling cloud. The twilight under snow is of surprising length, and the first stars seem to prolong it, shining like fierce gold flowers in the wastes of sky. And then, as the twilight lessens, the shining of the stars in the darkness above the snow creates the ultimate effect of loveliness. It brings about an effect of eternity: of eternal starlight and snowlight shining forever one against the other in the snowy darkness, reflecting each other, fixed in eternal wonder.

It is, in actuality, a brief wonder; and for us, quite a rare one also. For the Russian or the Austrian, the shining of stars on snow is a common event, whereas for us it occurs far more rarely than a rainbow. And whereas for the Russian the coming of snow and the ultimate coming of spring are as certain and fixed as dark and daylight, for us there is no certainty of snow or spring at all. There is instead the consolation of a score of little sudden springs before the spring itself, the knowledge that the snow will scarcely have created that paradise of whiteness and frost and silence and starlight before the primroses and the singing thrushes and the sun are beginning to destroy it again and create another.

PRIMROSES AND CATKINS

HERE, IMMEDIATELY AFTER A BLAST OF SNOW, there is a great change over the land. Like the November gale, the snow has some power of cleansing and rejuvenating; it cauterises, mercilessly burns out the lassitude of the winter-sick land. The earth, after snow, looks at once to have more life; it feels to have more life. It breaks easily in the hand, comes down at a touch from dead clots to living particles; it is suddenly dry and kindly, even warm. There is a raising of dust from harrows in fields. The air is brittle. It is suddenly easy to light fires in the open air, and now, wherever woods have been thinned, the smoke of fires clouds up and is gusted wildly away by wind, settling again, at evening, in long flat clouds like floating blue islands among the thinned trees. Woods that have been thinned have a surprising spaciousness, a new shape. Here, in the south, where woods seem to be grown for two purposes, spile-thinning and pheasant cover, a wood after nine or ten years begins to look like a man needing several haircuts. It becomes a little wild and barbaric and untidy, the earth spiritless from long seclusion from sunlight. Finally the young trees are ripe for cutting, and then, as they come down, new distances are formed, new contours, and the whole place has a new youth and a new spruceness, exactly like a man who has had his long-needed haircut at last.

And life is more forward in thinned woods, spring earlier. It is the response to light, to the magnetism of sky. Primroses appear miraculously on the cleared ground, in short-stemmed tufts that thicken rapidly. Here, we gather primroses all winter, even for Christmas Day. We have gathered them in January, by moonlight, when they seemed like flecks of earth-bound moonlight themselves. They seem extra precious, these winter primroses. Rain-blanched and small and frost-browned, they are often very poor; but they are symbolic. They are living bits of sunlight. They are indomitable. Nothing can suppress them. For such flimsy-petalled soft flowers they have an astonishing tenacity and toughness. They come up through the snow. They almost thrive on it: so that as the snow melts it seems to melt not into water but into flowers, into fresh tiny flower-flakes of palest yellow.

Violets are scarcer, more aristocratic. They lack that friendly indomitable toughness of the primrose. They have, more or less, a fixed season. They appear, in woods, in great purple lace carpets in April, in fine milky threads among the primroses. Long before them, lords-and-ladies are pushing up like bits of bright green glass, and honeysuckle leaves are unbuttoning along the wood ridings. Tassels of dog's mercury are greening the dark wood floors everywhere. Catkins are out. The circle is turning.

Until you begin to consider it, the season of catkins seems to be brief, to begin only with the first heat of the February sun and then to peter out as soon as Easter is past and the shadows of the woods are rejoining to thicken over the lank rosy-stemmed primroses. In reality it begins a good deal earlier – in fact as far back as September, before the leaves have turned – and goes on much later, not even ending with the yellow oak flowers in May or the red ash tree blooms, but only with the tender blanched-green tassels of the sweet chestnuts

in July. In fact this season of curious tree flowers covers more than half the English year, its spring beginning in January, its summer coming in April, its winter in the zenith of summer time.

It is quite a modest and precious blossoming. It is curious that in England it is the little trees, the doll trees as it were, that blossom bountifully and gorgeously, and the great trees that break into a sombre and unheeded flowering. No poet that I can call to mind has put himself into ecstasies over the ruby blossoms of the elm or into half the state of singing over the purple catkins of the alder that he keeps for the cherry and the rose. The catkin is a sort of Cinderella among flowers, not so much unwanted as unnoticed. The poet who lifts his eyes to the stars or lowers them for the flowers, the stars on earth, often misses as he does so the flowers that hang between earth and heaven, the delicate and unflashing constellations that light up the dark branches of wintry trees.

This season of tree blossoms always begins as far back as September, unheeded, with the little stiff hazel catkins, softest green and in shape like fairy sausages, very tight and secluded on the boughs among the brown-tipped nuts and the sapless leaves. The hazel is one of those rare trees that begin to blossom before its fruit has fallen, though the flower is only in bud and remains half seen and half opened until the tree is leafless. That opening comes at first with extreme slowness, imperceptibly, the catkins still stiff and green and often frost-reddened until the early days of January, the first days of the new light. Until that change and coming of the light the catkins push stiffly skyward, as though seeking it. No sooner does it come than they droop downwards, lengthening with inconceivable quickness, yellower and richer than ever the January sunlight will be. There is a time, just before February, when they hang half-stiff, half-loose, undancing and unbrilliant, no longer green and not yet golden. It is not their loveliest time but it is their most triumphant. They have broken through the winter and the darkness. It is an unpassionate blossoming, not to be compared with the bursting of the wild crab bloom or the rose, but it is pristine, the catkins are one with light, responsive to it and governed by it, the tassels richening and lengthening as the light itself enrichens and lengthens to fullest spring.

Beginning a little later and bursting into a later glory, the sallow comes into its spring with the hazel, so that often on warm spinney sides they light up each other, the silky mouse-silver of the sallow against the powdery half-gold of the hazel, the sallow buds like smooth cocoons, the hazel like yellowish caterpillars everlastingly suspended, the one unalterably motionless against the marionettish dangling and dancing of the other. Later the sallow rises to a glory, a glory of colour and fragrance, that the hazel never quite reaches. It is, with the daffodil, the true Easter flower, standing for the

ascension of sunlight, for the final triumph of light over the tomb of winter darkness.

It seems to me the most beautiful of all catkins, finer, even though it is so little different, than the willow, which comes a little later. Whereas the sallow comes late into leaf, the willow comes too soon, so that the leaves and flowers hide each other a little, producing an effect that is not green and not gold, a fine sight, but never so entrancing as that pure and transcendent blaze of gold into which the sallow bursts in April.

As with the hazel and the sallow, so it is with the alder and the birch – their catkins bud and blossom on naked branches, before the winter is past. And in that lies all their modest and delicate glory. On wet rain-dark winter days, when the sheep pens on the late rootland are still dreary with sludder and the grassland is sodden and lifeless, the birches in the wood down the lane come most suddenly and wonderfully to life. The rain, clinging to their delicate twigs and catkins, seems to undergo a transformation. It is as though the buds perform the miracle of turning the rain to wine, for with the red buds and redder catkins shining through its drops the rain gleams like dim burgundy.

Something of this happens also to the alder. But the alder branches never hold the raindrops as the birch twigs do, and the effect is not liquid but vapourish, and not red but purple – a strange haziness of purple shot with the tenderest orange-gold. The alder is a waterside tree and in the south often grows among the plantations of ash and sweet chestnut that grow up into the thick straight saplings which are cut down, every ten years or so, for stakes and hop poles. This work is done in winter, from November to February, and it quite often happens that in a waterside copse there are alders to be cut down with the ashes and chestnuts. Where the axe cuts it the ash wood is white and the chestnut almost as white, but the alder wood is a wonderful colour, a most vivid orange-gold, like the colour of tiger lilies, but even brighter. It is the same golden-orange colour exactly, but infinitely softened and diluted, which is mingled with the sombre purple of the catkins, which in turn is so like the purple of the coming leaves.

By the end of May the alder, like the birch and the hazel and the poplar and the sallow, is forgotten, overshadowed by the glory of oaks and beeches, the oaks with their pretty yellow tassels bringing the catkin season almost to an end. The end does not really come until July, until the flowering of the sweet chestnuts, when the pale green tassel flowers soften the hard gleaming light of the drooping leaves under the hot sunshine.

No sooner is it ended, however, than the hazels, breaking invisibly into tiniest catkins under the late summer leaves, are ready to begin again their brief winter, a winter that breaks into spring before the winter of all other life has half begun.

THE DARLING BUDS OF MARCH

AND COMING ALMOST HAND IN HAND with this catkin season there is another lovely aspect of spring, the phase of unopened buds. It is obscured again and again by the glories of crocus and primrose and daffodil, and if the weather is mild by the first blossoms of the flowering trees, which outshine it completely. The pink grace of the early almonds is not only lovely but easy to see. But the ruby buds of the birches are dark and obscure even in the March sunlight. The flowers of *Pyrus japonica* on the south walls of houses open wide and flame crimson with all the delicacy and purity of single roses. But the golden buds of willows are golden only in sudden and accidental angles of light or against backgrounds of stormy cloud. They shine even then with a gold that has no counterpart in the colours of flowers, but with the soft and sombre light of polished wood, as though the buds were shining splinters of golden walnut.

The phase, always brief, represents in a sense a prologue to spring and at the same time an epilogue to winter, belonging all the time to neither one nor the other. The buds are awake but not open; they are no longer dead but still not alive. They have lost the colourlessness of winter, but there is no greenness in them. They are part of a kind of vernal twilight, a between season, a little interlude between one large act and another, an interlude that is all over and obscured and forgotten by the time the cuckoo is calling in the flowering ash trees.

Yet while it lasts, and however the weather may turn and change, from snow to sunlight or frost to rain, it seems to me to hold as much of the heart of spring as the almond and the daffodil. The south-west rain may smash and tear the crocuses like so many inside-out umbrellas to a ruin of gold and purple and white, but the rain profits the dark copses of birch and hazel and sweet chestnut so that they take on fresh beauty and life. The trees are liquid with colour. They stand drenched in wine-red or mauve or olive rain, the buds colouring the drops and the rain in turn richening the colour of the buds, so that the whole woodside gleams with the liquid passionate glow of multitudinous rain-drenched branches. And if the sun breaks out the rain against the buds is like still silver, or like blown beads of silver if the wind springs up. Whatever happens the buds, washed and slightly more rounded and swollen by the fresh rain, become glorified. Unlike the crocus or the daffodils or even the almonds, neither rain nor wind nor frost desolates them. They are fragile but strong. The buds of beech are like slender varnished chrysalises lying in light but secure sleep along the grey twigs. The buds of oak are like fat hard knobs of leather. The first buds of elm are little fluffy French knots of dark pink wool securely sewn on the jagged branches. The grey-black buds of the ash are like arrow heads of iron. They all have the common virtues of strength and delicacy.

They all share a kind of delicate and subdued beauty. Individually they are no more than charming miniature shapes in dim pink or olive or mauve or grey or sepia. But collectively, in still or sunlit or wind-tossed multitudes, they transform the tree itself into a single colossal swaying and shining bud, an immense burning emblem of spring half-wakened.

And if this is very true of the larger trees and of the trees that grow naturally in great groups of one or many kinds, oaks and elms and beeches and sweet chestnut and birches,

it is perhaps even truer of the lesser and rarer trees, sycamores and willows and alders and wild cherries and beams and maples, whose buds have also the virtue of a greater individual loveliness. The buds of the sycamore are full silk shapes of creamy pink when young; there is something sweet and milky and virginal about them. And the maple buds, though so very like them, are smaller and less pink and silky. The wild cherry buds are gathered in little knots like brown beans at the tip of the smooth satin stems and on the hedges the buds of hawthorn and blackthorn, earliest to break, are like little beads of wine and cream. And in gardens and orchards the buds of peach and apple and pear are like taut nipples of pink dove-colour and white, full of the milk of coming flower.

And loveliest of all, the young alder. Cut down, the alder shoots up again, like the sallow and the ash and the sweet chestnut,

with new long wands of sombre purple. The wood is too young
to flower, but the leaf buds themselves have the shapely loveliness
and enchantment of flowers just breaking, unfurling out of the bare
stem like petals of smoky mauve, a strange rare colour, unbrilliant
but rich, quiet but burning, that resembles the colour of sun-faded
violets. There is a kind of bloom over the buds of the young alder, a
soft cloudiness, which no other tree buds ever seem to possess, but
which is something peculiar to flowers of mauve and purple and
lilac. There is the same mistiness of lovely bloom on the petals of
summer irises, on the silky silver cups of pasque flowers, on clematis
and campanulas and mauve geraniums and the dark unopened buds

of lilac itself. It is the bloom of the plum and the grape and the wild sloe. There is something autumnal about it. So that the buds of the alder, so dark and soft and rich, seem to belong to another world, to be almost out of place among the pale colours and half-colours and gentle light and nakedness of first spring. They burn with the smoky darkness of some autumn fire.

And at the beginning of March, at the height of their beauty, it is suddenly as though their lilac smoke is spirited through all the wood and copses. The million buds of birch and hazel and chestnut and oak are suddenly on fire. The smoke is dark and still under cloud and rain, and then tawny in the sunlight and then still tawnier and richer and warmer as the days go past, until finally the sunlight starts it into an immense gold and emerald flame that spreads and intensifies until every bud on every tree is a green candle against the April sky.

And as the flame burns more fiercely and wonderfully the buds are consumed. The polished brown husks of the beeches fall down like ashes on the copper lawn of dead husks and leaves. The elm drops warm soft showers of fluffy fire. Ash and oak break into a flowering of mahogany and yellow, the wild cherry stands transfigured in white. The willows are turned to balloons of emerald, the horse chestnut is glorious with pale brown flower buds like those of Victorian wool, and Zacchaeus could hide again in the sycamore. And the alder, once so splendid with purple fire, stands utterly insignificant, the purple gone, the tawny catkins withered, a little dark widow of a tree along the watersides, and buds everywhere are gone and forgotten as though they had never been.

THE CIRCLE IS TURNED

THE CIRCLE HAS BEEN TURNED, and the wood has turned with it. It has flowered and died and renewed itself. It has been stripped and scorched, thinned and pillaged, and yet remains. It is the most constantly beautiful object about the countryside. There are times when fields look dead, when gardens and their houses are dreary with desolation. The wood has no single minute of eclipse throughout the year. It turns not only a circle, but a circle of perpetual loveliness. It never fades, never cheats. It has mystery but not falsity. It is staunch and even majestic but never overpowering. It is a place of quiet and conflict, of absolute peace and tigerish bloodiness, of passion and death. It is a contrast of power and delicacy, space and littleness. Yet all the time, throughout the year, it has its own special atmosphere. You have only to walk a yard under the trees in order to become under its spell, to sense the change, the sometimes startling, sometimes soothing difference in the spirit of the air. There is some precious quality brought about by the close gathering together of trees into a wood that defies analysis. The mere planting together of trees will not create it. An avenue will not do it, nor a park, nor an orchard. There must, it seems, be a closeness, an untidiness, a wildness. There must be all kinds of trees, all kinds of flowers and creatures, a conflicting and yet harmonious pooling of life. A wood planted, as fox coverts often are, with one kind of tree, has no life at all. It stands dead as a wood of hop poles. It is the wood of little and great trees, of flowers and water, of squirrel and fox, bird and badger, of light and shadowiness, that has the everlasting vibration of life in it, that special rare atmosphere, at once soothing and refreshing and somehow elevating, that only the best of woods can give.

Woods like that stand about the English countryside in scores and hundreds – even, I suppose, in thousands. They are oases of wildlife in a too-ordered, too-civilised country. They are the green islands left high and dry by the waters of town and suburb. In so small a country they are trebly precious. Without them the English countryside, man-made for the greater part, would be nothing.

To that eternal question 'Where shall we go?' they have in fact supplied the best of all answers: through the woods.

Shall we go?

Little Toller Books

We publish old and new writing attuned to nature and the landscape, working with a wide range of the very best writers and artists. We pride ourselves on publishing affordable books of the highest quality. If you have enjoyed this book, you will also like exploring our other titles.

Anthology
ARBOREAL: WOODLAND WORDS
CORNERSTONES: SUBTERRANEAN WRITING

Field Notes
MY HOME IS THE SKY: THE LIFE OF J. A. BAKER *Hetty Saunders*
DEER ISLAND *Neil Ansell*
ORISON FOR A CURLEW *Horatio Clare*
SOMETHING OF HIS ART: WALKING WITH J. S. BACH *Horatio Clare*
LOVE, MADNESS, FISHING *Dexter Petley*
WATER AND SKY *Neil Sentance*
THE TREE *John Fowles*

New Nature Monographs
HERBACEOUS *Paul Evans*
ON SILBURY HILL *Adam Thorpe*
THE ASH TREE *Oliver Rackham*
MERMAIDS *Sophia Kingshill*
BLACK APPLES OF GOWER *Iain Sinclair*
BEYOND THE FELL WALL *Richard Skelton*
LIMESTONE COUNTRY *Fiona Sampson*
HAVERGEY *John Burnside*
SNOW *Marcus Sedgwick*
LANDFILL *Tim Dee*
SPIRITS OF PLACE *Sara Maitland*

Nature Classics Library
THROUGH THE WOODS *H. E. Bates*
MEN AND THE FIELDS *Adrian Bell*
THE MIRROR OF THE SEA *Joseph Conrad*
ISLAND YEARS, ISLAND FARM *Frank Fraser Darling*
THE MAKING OF THE ENGLISH LANDSCAPE *W. G. Hoskins*
BROTHER TO THE OX *Fred Kitchen*
FOUR HEDGES *Clare Leighton*
DREAM ISLAND *R. M. Lockley*
THE UNOFFICIAL COUNTRYSIDE *Richard Mabey*
RING OF BRIGHT WATER *Gavin Maxwell*
EARTH MEMORIES *Llewelyn Powys*
IN PURSUIT OF SPRING *Edward Thomas*
THE NATURAL HISTORY OF SELBORNE *Gilbert White*

LITTLE TOLLER BOOKS
Lower Dairy, Toller Fratrum, Dorset DT2 oEL
W. littletoller.co.uk **E.** books@littletoller.co.uk